Humanistic
Consulting

ALSO BY DAVID NOER

Humanistic Consulting

Its History, Philosophy and Power for Organizations

DAVID NOER

McFarland & Company, Inc., Publishers
Jefferson, North Carolina

ISBN (print) 978-1-4766-6779-9
ISBN (ebook) 978-1-4766-2747-2

LIBRARY OF CONGRESS CATALOGUING DATA ARE AVAILABLE

BRITISH LIBRARY CATALOGUING DATA ARE AVAILABLE

Front cover image © 2017 iStock

Manufactured in the United States of America

*McFarland & Company, Inc., Publishers
Box 611, Jefferson, North Carolina 28640
www.mcfarlandpub.com*

Table of Contents

Table of Contents

List of Figures

Preface

I recently interviewed a candidate to help conduct a leadership development workshop. "I use a humanistic approach," I began.

After a pause and a quizzical look she said, "I like to work with people, too."

"That's nice because the participants in our workshop are all people, no dogs or robots allowed," I responded, attempting to inject a little humor. "Tell me about your humanistic values and contrast them with those of a traditional management consultant."

She replied by telling me about her experience in team-building and familiarity with diagnostic tools such as the Myers-Briggs type indicator, the FIRO-B, and certification on a popular 360-degree feedback instrument.

"What did you learn about yourself when you last experienced a T-group and do you think NTL is losing its influence?"

She'd never gone through one of those "useless, embarrassing, sensitivity training sessions," and didn't think they were worth the effort. She admitted she'd never heard of the National Training Labs.

This candidate had a master's degree in organization development, a field grounded and differentiated by humanistic values. She was bright, motivated, and excited about working in leadership development. Unfortunately she was reflective of too many humanistic practitioners—clueless as to the history and evolution of her field, and focused on tools and techniques at the expense of the primary tools: her own compassion, empathy, and authenticity.

A few months later, a senior executive in a large corporation, was seeking to retain a coach to "fix" one of his employees who was "not a team player," had "problems with authority" but was "loved" by his own employees and customers.

After the normal ice-breaking small talk, I finally asked the essential questions, "To what degree do you think you are part of the problem? Are you willing to examine your own behavior? Can I count on you to meet with this employee and me to make the relationship more productive?"

"No, no, you've got it wrong. I want to hire a coach for *him*—give him feedback on what changes *he* needs to make."

"Does he think he needs a coach?"

"No, but I do, and you have to let him know why."

"So, you'd be the client, not him. Have I got that right?"

From there, the session went downhill rapidly. I left, knowing that this executive needed to retain a coach not grounded in values of openness, free will, and collaboration, and dubious that such a coach would achieve much. I was also quite sure that the executive would be telling his HR vice president not to send him any more of those touchy-feely, ex-hippie kooks masquerading as executive coaches.

The Purpose of This Book

These two experiences, along with many others in my professional life, clarified the vital need for both practitioner and client to better understand the history, focus, and value base of humanistic consultation. Far too many practitioners have little understanding of the roots and evolution of the core values of their field. Far too many operating managers lose the powerful value of humanistic consultation by seeking simple, external, prescriptive solutions to complex problems involving human relationships.

The humanistic approach to working with individuals and organizations spans leadership development, executive coaching, organization development practice, organizational behavior teaching, and efforts to transform and revitalize entire organizational systems. Its tools and techniques are borrowed from clinical psychology, counseling, therapeutic approaches, and business change strategies. In the final analysis, the most relevant humanistic tool is the practitioners own warm body—her compassion, empathy, core values, and authenticity. The historical roots of humanistic consulting practice, its cross-functional applications, and its powerful potential have, for too long, gone unexamined. Their articulation is the purpose of this book.

Audiences

Humanistic practitioners. This book will be helpful to both internal and external humanistic consultants regardless of the focus of their practice. It traces the historical roots and overlapping disciplines of their profession.

It will clarify the sources of their interventions and provide a holistic perspective that will enable them to better serve their clients and affirm the core values of their calling.

Managers seeking consultants. For managers seeking consulting assistance, understanding the differences between the roles of traditional management consultants and those of the humanistic variety will eliminate confusion and surprises. Awareness of the values and approaches of humanistic consultants will greatly facilitate consultant choice, depth of intervention, and client involvement.

Managers wanting to operate in a humanistic manner. Operational managers attempting to move from a controlling, evaluating, prescribing, role to an individual or group helping relationship will gain a deeper understanding of the skill and value orientation of the new approach. They will realize the wisdom of partnering with an experienced humanistic consultant to guide them through the transition.

Those in leadership development roles. Regardless of functional orientation, those seeking to develop organizational leaders with the interpersonal competence and intra-personal insight to build sustainable, productive, socially responsible organizations will find this book of great benefit. Humanistic approaches to leadership development are central to nurturing leaders with the abilities to be relevant to today's complex, multicultural, global organizations. Traditional training and development methodologies will only result in traditional, marginally effective leaders.

Students, researchers, and organizational historians. The book provides fresh insights into the historical roots and interconnectedness of the humanistic consulting model. Without understanding the evolution, scope, and potential of humanistic consulting, students, teachers, and researchers will be operating without an anchor to the past or a compass to the future.

Overview of the Contents

"Part One: History, Evolution and Applications"—the chapters in this section trace the history, interconnectedness, and application areas of humanistic consulting practice:

Chapter 1, "The Humanistic Consultant," covers the definition of the field, its relationship to traditional management consulting, and characteristics of practitioners.

Chapter 2, "Organization Development: A Concept in Search of a

Definition," traces early attempts to define planned change, the notion of OD as a religion, and the field's foundational values.

Chapter 3, "The Beginning: Three Wise Men and the Birth of NTL," covers the influence of Kurt Lewin, the values of the three founders of the National Training Labs, and the contribution of NTL to humanistic practice.

Chapter 4, "The Formative Years: Outsiders, Stems, Roots and Streams," reviews the growth of NTL, the development of the T-group, the influence of the Tavistock Institute, and the theoretical roots planted by Maslow and McGregor.

Chapter 5, "The OD Practitioner," covers the characteristics and potential threats to the practitioner, the necessity of marginality, and the need to partner with HR and line managers.

Chapter 6, "Organizational Behavior: OD's Academic Cousin," traces the parallel growth of OB teaching and research, the contribution of the Harvard Business School, and the differences between OB and OD.

Chapter 7, "Organization Transformation: OD's Radical Cousin," reviews the thrust for societal transformation through organizations, the evolution to economic business-based transformation and the trend toward large system interventions.

Chapter 8, "Humanistic Coaching," covers the growing application of humanistic practice to executive and managerial coaching, the primary coaching derailment factors, the triangle coaching model, and the power of organizational truth tellers.

Chapter 9, "Leadership Development," emphasizes the need to focus on leadership competencies that are compatible with humanistic values, threats to practitioner authenticity, and methods of adding developmental value.

"Part Two: Influence of Therapeutic and Philosophic Models"—the chapters in this section analyze the impact of therapeutic techniques and existential philosophy on humanistic practice.

Chapter 10, "Reflections on Therapy and Consultation," highlights the fuzzy boundaries between therapeutic and consultation techniques and introduces a model of therapeutic approaches.

Chapter 11, "The Big Three: Freud and His Dissident Disciples," covers the therapeutic approaches of Freud, Adler, and Jung, outlines their intervention strategies, and discusses implications for the practitioner.

Chapter 12, "A Discordant Quartet: Perls, Rogers, Ellis and Skinner," contrasts the approaches of Gestalt, Person-Centered, Rational-Emotive, and Behavioral interventions and reflects on their implications for the practitioner. The chapter ends with a chart outlining the relationship of the major therapeutic approaches to humanistic practice.

Chapter 13, "The Existential Influence," covers the impact of existential theory on the three dimensions of Argyris' intervention model, the existential imperative for marginality, and Kierkegaard's leap of faith as a way to understand practitioner adherence to humanistic values.

"Part Three: Perspectives and Observations"—the chapters in this part offer ideas, perspectives, and observations on humanistic practice.

Chapter 14, "Reflections and Heretical Realities," postulates ten deceptively simple realities and reflects upon their impact on OB, OD, and OT.

Chapter 15, "Six Managerial Paradigms in the Process of Becoming," uses philosopher Georg Hegel's theory to frame leadership and managerial paradigms in terms of what was—what is—and what is in the process of becoming, and speculates on the implications to the practitioner.

Chapter 16, "The Practitioner as a Hired Gun," uses the metaphor of an old west gunslinger to examine the practitioner's tendency to be a "lone ranger," the danger of staying too long and becoming worse than the problem he came to clean up, and the possibility of becoming trapped in a fraudulent role.

Chapter 17, "Breaking Organizational Codependency," explains the toxic consequences of employees with codependent relationships with organizations and outlines strategies for the practitioner to help break codependent organizational relationships.

Chapter 18, "Nurturing Learning Cultures," offers strategies for the practitioner to help build a learning culture and guidelines for promoting learning cultures in troubled times.

Chapter 19, "New Reality Management," traces the evolution of the old psychological employment contract to the new, and offers advice and guidelines to the manager for relevant ways to accommodate new reality conceptualizations of loyalty, motivation, and commitment.

Chapter 20, "The Right Stuff," gives advice, offers strategies for becoming and remaining a relevant humanistic practitioner, and provides guidelines for unleashing the power of applied human spirit.

The three appendices are comprised of self-assessment tools mentioned in Chapters 17, 19 and 20. Appendix A contains the Susceptibility to Organizational Codependence Index, Appendix B is the Organizational Preference Questionnaire, and Appendix C is the Consulting Behaviors Inventory. Readers and practitioners are encouraged to utilize these with their relevant chapters.

PART ONE

HISTORY, EVOLUTION AND APPLICATIONS

"We are not makers of history. We are made by history."
—*Martin Luther King, Jr.*

As Dr. King reminds us, we are shaped by past values, cultures, and beliefs. The humanistic approach to the formation of organizational and individual helping relationships rests upon the conceptual shoulders of those theoreticians and practitioners who have come before us. The work of the humanistic practitioner—be she in a managerial or consultation role—is much more relevant and personally meaningful when informed by an appreciation of the contributions and values of those who formed the field.

The chapters in this section differentiate humanistic consultation and management practice from the more traditional approaches. They outline fundamental humanistic values and trace the evolution of organization development practice and organizational behavior research. The humanistic approaches to organization transformation, managerial coaching, and leadership development are explored.

1. The Humanistic Consultant

"The soft side is actually the hard side."
—*humanistic consultant*

In order to understand the unique perspective of humanistic consulting it's necessary to differentiate it from traditional management consulting. The points of departure are illustrated by a conversation between two of my friends—a vice president of a large corporation, and a self-employed organization development consultant. The consultant was attempting to explain why she turned down a lucrative engagement with a multinational corporation.

"They wanted me to study their new college graduate turnover problem, write a report with recommendations, present it to their executive committee, and leave the next steps in their hands. I would have accumulated a pile of billable hours and made a lot of money but I walked away."

"Why wouldn't you take that assignment? It sounds perfect—analyze the problem, make a recommendation, send them a bill and ride off into the sunset without getting bogged down with any of the implementation headaches," said the vice president.

"That's not the kind of consulting I do," she replied. "I help clients diagnose core issues, work with them discover to what extent their own behavior is part of the problem and support them as they work through personal and organizational change."

"Oh, yeah," said the vice president. "I forgot. You're one of those touchy-feely, types. I'll bet you even do some of those sensitivity group love-ins. I can't believe organizations actually pay for all that soft-side crap."

"T-groups are not 'love-ins.' Most participants find them to be one of the most personally powerful and organizationally relevant sessions they've ever attended. I don't do client sensitivity training but I do use some of the things I learned about myself in T-groups to help clients.

What you call the *soft side*, is actually the *hard side*, because it takes enormous courage to stand back, look at yourself and your organization in the mirror, assess what you see without distorting filters, and muster up the courage and will to make needed changes."

"Still sounds soft and fuzzy to me—not what we pay consultants to do in my company," said the vice president.

Differences Between Humanistic and Traditional Management Consulting

It took two stories and a round of drinks to mellow out a potentially dysfunctional relationship between two very talented people. I used the following two "tales" to inject some needed humor and illustrate the stereotypes of these two forms of consulting.

A Traditional Management Consulting Tale

A shepherd was herding his flock in a remote pasture when suddenly a brand new BMW advanced out of a dust cloud. The driver, a young man in a Baroni suit, Gucci shoes, Ray Ban sunglasses and YSL tie, leaned out the window and asked the shepherd, "If I tell you exactly how many sheep you have in your flock, will you give me one?" The shepherd looked at the man, then looked at his peacefully grazing flock and calmly answered, "Sure."

The man parked his car, whipped out his iPad, surfed to a NASA site, called up a satellite, scanned the area, and opened a spreadsheet. In a few minutes he received an email response. Finally, he printed a 130-page report on his miniaturized printer, gave it to the shepherd, and said, "You have exactly 1,586 sheep."

"That is correct. Take one of the sheep," said the shepherd. He watched the young man select one of the animals, bundle it into his car and said, "If I can tell you exactly what your business is, will you give me back my animal?"

"Okay, why not?" answered the young man.

"Clearly, you are a management consultant," said the shepherd.

"That's right," said the man. "But how did you guess that?"

"No guessing required," said the shepherd. "You turned up here although nobody called you. You want to get paid for an answer I already knew to a question I never asked, and you don't know crap about my business. Now give me back my dog!"

Humanistic Consulting Tale

A humanistic executive coach grounded in non-directive empathy and the Rogerian approach of acceptance and unconditional positive regard is having a conversation with a client in his corner office atop a skyscraper.

"My business is bankrupt and I'm going to lose everything I've worked for," says the executive.

"Sounds like you're feeling sad," responds the coach.

"My wife is leaving me and taking the kids with her."

"You're losing a lot," says the coach.

"I'm totally depressed."

"You're feeling depressed," says the coach in an empathetic voice.

"I'm going to kill myself."

"You want to kill yourself," states the coach.

"I'm going to do it right now," says the executive.

"I notice you're walking toward the window," says the coach.

The executive opens the window and stands on the ledge. "I'm going to jump," he says.

"You're about to jump out the window," the coach calmly states, raising from his chair.

The executive leaps out the window and is plummeting to the sidewalk when he looks up, sees the coach and hears him shouting down through cupped hands. "I—notice—you've—jumped."

What makes these two tales humorous is that there is a degree of truth in each. The middle manager who defines a traditional management consultant as, "someone from out of town with a briefcase who thinks she knows more than me and is paid more," has a point. Top executives sometimes retain external consultants without picking the brains of their own employees. The message to bypassed managers is that, despite what they know, they're doomed never to be prophets in their own land. New, relatively inexperienced MBAs are paid generous salaries and bonuses by international management consulting firms and sometimes perform routine, formula-based analytical work.

There is also some truth in the other tale. Humanistic consultants of all persuasions—organization development practitioners, executive coaches, leadership developers, and those seeking to transform organizational systems—too often get bogged down in techniques and obscure language at the expense of action and clarity. There are a surprising number who figuratively let their clients jump out the window by overdosing on empathy and ignoring action.

THE TRANSFORMATIVE POTENTIAL OF HUMANISTIC PRACTICE

Of the two approaches, humanistic consulting is the least understood and frequently the least accepted. Its core values of free will, collaboration, client responsibility, participation, and openness, often operate against the grain of corporate cultures. Its value is marginalized at the expense of its enormous transformative potential. Although there are consultants operating under a hybrid model, the differences depicted in figure 1, make it difficult to consistently bridge the gap.

Figure 1

Traditional management and humanistic consulting

Traditional management consulting	Humanistic consulting
Doctor-patient model.	Collaborative model.
Consultant plays expert role. Client plays dependent role.	Consultant plays partnership role. Client and consultant have interdependent roles.
Consultant primarily driven by values of measurement, efficiency & client compliance.	Consultant primarily driven by values of participation, inclusion, and client free choice.
Analytical orientation.	Helping orientation.
Focus on data and predictability.	Focus on change and sustainability.
Product is a report, specific recommendations, & step-by-step implementation plan.	Product is individual and system insight, facilitative guidance & support.
Consultant has no professional obligation to become involved in implementation.	Consultant professionally driven to facilitate implementation.

Characteristics of Humanistic Practitioners

Don't work by formula or prescription. Although sometimes found in "change management" silos of large, traditional management consulting organizations, humanistic consultants are not a smooth fit. They frequently find themselves operating in unnatural prescriptive modes. Humanistic consultants don't work by formula, don't view their product as a report or a series of recommendations, and are as concerned with values, inclusion, openness, human potential, and process as with financial ratios. They are sometimes pejoratively labeled as "touchy-feely," or representative of the "soft side," yet when organizational leaders reflect on who has most impacted their lives, their careers, and their sense of purpose, they nearly always name a humanistic consultant.

Eclectic backgrounds bonded by galvanizing characteristics. Humanistic consultation is an eclectic endeavor and successful practitioners come from a variety of backgrounds. Some, like many of their traditional management consultant cousins, have MBAs or business undergraduate degrees while others have training in clinical, developmental, industrial/organizational, and other branches of psychology. The backgrounds of competent humanistic practitioners are, however, not limited to these fields. Their training and orientation encompass a wide range of liberal arts, social and behavioral sciences. Diverse though their backgrounds may be, they have two powerful common galvanizing characteristics: they are able to form client-centered helping relationships, and believe in the potential of positive human change.

Can include operating managers. Operating managers—sometimes called "line" managers to distinguish them from staff functionaries—can also function as humanistic manager/practitioners. This can be an exceptionally useful role but one that requires a difficult balancing act and can be greatly facilitated by guidance from an experienced humanistic consultant.

Preponderance of lone-wolves. Even though they practice their profession inside formal organizations, a surprising number of humanistic consultants are counter-dependent to organizational power and control—the more they experience power and control, the more they rebel—and, therefore, work as individual lone-wolf contractors. When they do form affiliative relationships they usually create small, boutique firms. Some work inside large, hierarchical organizations as "internal consultants" and must continually struggle to maintain the necessary marginality to be effective.

Humanistic consultants work under labels such as organization development practitioners, executive/management coaches, leadership developers, and organizational behavior teachers and researchers. These labels are deceptive, ambiguous, and often limiting. The values, interventions, and historical roots overlap and refute separation, artificial boundaries, and narrow certification requirements. Their interconnectivity, history, positive potential, and unique differentiation from traditional management consulting require deeper understanding by both client and consultant.

The Foundational Basis of Humanistic Practice

There are four ideological columns that support humanistic practice. All are necessary, but the most fundamental is the concept of humanism and its core values.

THE FOUR PILLARS OF HUMANISTIC PRACTICE

The philosophy and values of humanism. Of humanism's many definitions, one of the most clear and cogent is found in the bylaws of the International Humanist Ethical Union (2002 1.2):

> Humanism is a democratic and ethical life stance which affirms that human beings have the right and responsibility to give meaning and shape to their own lives. It stands for the building of a more humane society through an ethic based on human and other natural values in the spirit of reason and free inquiry through human capabilities. It is not theistic, and it does not accept supernatural views of reality.

Although this definition excludes a religious connotation and the concept of "secular humanism," comes with philosophical baggage for some, humanistic consulting as used in this book, is neither anti-religious nor pro-atheistic. It is, however, anti-dogmatic, and pro-human potential. Successful humanistic practitioners represent a wide variety of religious orientations. Their humanism is not based on rejecting religion or denying God.

THE TRANSFORMATIVE POTENTIAL OF HUMANISTIC PRACTICE

Humanistic psychology, existential philosophy, and therapeutic techniques. As will be addressed in Part Two, the second supportive column is a combination of ideas from humanistic psychology, existential philosophy and therapeutic techniques. The foundations of humanistic psychology were constructed by theorists such as Abraham Maslow (1968), who emphasized a hierarchy of needs and motivations leading to self-actualization, and the client-centered therapeutic approach of Carl Rogers (1961) who postulated that an accepting environment and unconditional positive regard would lead to client growth and development. The core principle of existentialism—that people have the freedom to define their purpose and meaning—is a primary value of humanistic consulting practice.

The extension of individual helping relationships to group interventions. The third foundational pillar is the migration of therapeutic processes to organizational systems. The classic articulation of this pillar was formulated by organization development pioneer Chris Argyris (1970). He used the term "interventionist," not consultant, when he outlined the three primary tasks of the consultant/interventionist: the generation of valid data, the client option of free choice, and the facilitation of client internal commitment. These three ingredients—valid data, free choice, internal commitment—are the central ingredients of today's humanistic consulting tool kit. Their roots and values can be traced to humanism and humanistic psychology. Argyris (p. 16), when addressing the relationship of the consultant to the client system, articulates the fundamental humanistic consulting value of client empowerment and lack of practitioner dependency:

> Our view ... focuses on how to maintain, or increase, the client system's autonomy; how to differentiate even more clearly the boundaries between the client system and the intervenor; and how to conceptualize and define the client system's health independently of the intervenor's. This view values the client system as an ongoing, self-responsible unity that has the obligation to be in control of its own destiny. An intervenor, in this view, assists a system to become more effective in problem solving, decision making, and decision implementation in such a way that the system can continue to be increasingly effective in these activities and have a decreasing need for the intervenor.

Concurrent with the extension of individual humanistic processes to groups and entire organizational systems, was the involvement of consultants/interventionists who were not licensed therapists or psychologists. Although there are a number of both licensed and unlicensed psychologists—industrial/organizational, clinical, counseling, and other varieties— in the field, the majority of practitioners have other credentials and experiential backgrounds. Most of today's humanistic consultants don't do or contract for therapeutic relationships but they—often without knowing the origins—use some of the humanistic therapeutic tools and processes.

Rejection of the "doctor-patient" and "pair-of-hands" consulting models. The final pillar involves the role of the consultant. In the doctor-patient model, the consultant assumes the role of expert, takes personal responsibility for diagnosing the client's problem, and prescribes actions and solutions. This often takes the form of writing a report, making a presentation, or outlining and recommending a detailed course of action. Humanistic consulting involves joint diagnosis, mutual discovery, client responsibility, and consultant coaching, facilitation, and feedback.

In the pair-of-hands role, the consultant loses her important differentiating marginality and becomes a surrogate employee, acting as an extension of the client manager. This relationship is described by Block (2000 24):

> Here the manager sees the consultant as an extra "pair-of-hands." The manager says, in effect, "I have neither the time nor the inclination to deal with this problem.

I have examined the deficiencies and have prepared an outline of what needs to be done. I want you to get it done as soon as possible." The manager retains full control. The consultant is expected to apply specialized knowledge to implement action plans toward the achievement of goals that the manager has defined.

Humanistic consultants add value by empowering the client, not by acting as a pseudo-employee or an outside expert. Often, because of their past experience, discomfort with collaboration and fear of vulnerability, clients attempt to pigeonhole consultants into these roles. Effective consultants find ways to avoid them and wise clients discover the power of mutual bonding around the valid data, free choice, internal commitment model.

Advice and Recommendations

- There is a fundamental difference between humanistic consulting and traditional management consulting. Some of the dimensions overlap and there are hybrid practitioners but there are clear points of departure.

- If you are a consultant who values (a) open collaborative client relationships; (b) are comfortable with a helping, empowering focus, and; (c) doesn't prescribe and gives clients free choice: you're at the humanistic side of the spectrum. If you (a) position yourself as an expert; (b) see analysis and prescription as the currency of your realm, and; (c) have an aversion to "soft, touchy-feely stuff," you are on the traditional management consulting end. Both approaches add value but it's difficult to effectively serve two paradigmatic masters and you need to be clear with yourself and your clients.

- If you're looking to retain a consultant be very clear on what you need and what you're buying. If you want a report, expert advice, and concrete external recommendations, retain a traditional consultant. If you're willing to put your own skin in the game, invest your feelings and emotions in the process, and collaborate in sometimes uncomfortable but necessary change, sign up with a humanist. Do your due diligence because if you retain one variety and want the other, you and your consultant will be disappointed.

- If you are a humanistic consultant and work inside a corporate structure, you will need to work very hard to maintain the necessary marginality to be effective. If your budget and your ego will let you, it is always a good idea to partner with an external. The outsider will learn from your perspective, and you'll benefit from her outside perspective.

- I use the term "consultant" generically. It can be the customary helping and advisory role but it also applies to executive coaches, leadership developers, and all other varieties of "truth tellers."

2. Organization Development: A Concept in Search of a Definition

"OD begins to make sense to me only when viewed as a
secular religion."—*Marvin Weisbord*

If there is one field—although its diverse techniques and levels of application defy strict categorization as a "field"—that is a natural home to the application of humanism to organizations, it is organization development (OD). This is because OD is grounded in humanistic core values and almost all practitioners engage in some form of consulting. To clarify a common labeling error, the name is *organization*, not *organizational* development. The founders meant to document their movement from a focus on developing individuals to one of developing organizations. So, in Scherer, Alban, and Weisbord's words (2016 33): "Please, everyone, from now on, call our field organization development. Please drop the 'al,' okay?"

Why OD Operates Under the Radar

For a field that has a large international network membership, offers a wide variety of master's and doctoral degrees, and distributes several practitioner-oriented publications and a refereed journal, OD operates surprisingly under the radar of many organizational leaders. In an informal sample of 400 MBA students with an average of over five years of business experience, I found less than ten percent were familiar with the term organization development. Of those who knew OD stood for something more than drug overdosing, several associated it with a fuzzy fringe of human resources, not something they viewed as central to the mainstream of business management.

Paradoxically, in testimony to the power of humanistic consultation, when seasoned organizational leaders describe the person external to their own chain of command who has been the most helpful in their development as a leader and as a person, they most often describe an OD consultant of either the internal or external variety. One reason for the lack of recognition is that many humanistic practitioners don't use the organization development label. They identify themselves by terms such as management or leadership developers, team builders or executive coaches. In some organizations, OD is erroneously seen as a surviving relic of the cult-like fringes of the 1960s human potential movement and wise practitioners simply avoid the label. A second reason for the disconnect between experienced leaders and MBA students involves differences in roles by level. MBA students are either in, or headed toward, technical and professional roles, while senior executives are in roles where leadership and personal, as opposed to technical, skills are the relevant competencies.

The Oxymoron of Planned Change: A Definitional Dilemma

Since organization development is one of the primary application areas of humanistic values in organizational systems, and since humanistic values manifest themselves in a variety of contexts, it is little wonder that there is definitional confusion. What exactly is this thing called organization development? What are its boundaries? How can it be accurately defined? Why are humanists attracted to it? These questions began nearly 70 years ago when the field started and are still with us today. The answers are elusive and have much to do with the field's eclectic nature and oxymoronic mission. Most practitioners, when pressed for a definition, come up with some variant of the concept of "planned change." Taking that phrase literally, planned change ranks right up there with other classic oxymorons such as airline food, military intelligence, and in today's environment, political correctness. The varied nature of the field and the intentional disregard for traditional disciplinary boundaries by many influential practitioners is both intriguing and frustrating to those conditioned to well-defined arenas of research and practice.

An Historic Book of Readings

A classic documentation of the heterogeneous, multi-dimensional nature of OD is found in an early book of readings edited by Bennis,

Benne and Chin (1961) with the oxymoronic title, *The Planning of Change*. Vaill (2009 5) documents its historical significance: "This book did as much or more than any other to articulate what the field of Organization Development might be. While individual readings are somewhat dated, the editors' various section introductions can still be read for basic original ideas about planning organizational change and consulting."

All of the contributions are over fifty years old and, in a field as young as organization development, constitute an historian's treasure chest of concepts, models, and processes that trace their roots to humanism. Here is Bennis on the typology of change, Shepard on early T-groups, and Lewin on quasi-stationary equilibria. Here too are Rogers, McGregor, both Ron and Gordon Lippitt, and Elliot Jaques. One can even find Timothy Leary and Will Schutz among the contributors. For the student of organization development history, the book is a prime resource, but it still leaves the answer to what exactly constitutes planned change unresolved. The reader is left with a feeling that grasping the concept is a bit like "getting religion." Once you get it, you've arrived but you can't explain how you got there or what it is that being there is. One prominent OD thought leader reinforced that perception by concluding that, to him, organization development was a type of secular religion.

Weisbord's Tortuous Historical Definitional Pilgrimage

A contemporary, somewhat antiseptic but academically palatable, definition of organization development is offered by Cummings and Worley (2015 2) when they write that it is "...a system-wide application and transfer of behavioral science knowledge to the planned development, improvement, and reinforcement of the strategies, structures, and process that lead to organization effectiveness."

A definition with more emotional resonance and a more direct connection to the humanistic paradigm was offered by Weisbord (1977 8) nearly forty years ago when he wrote: "OD begins to make sense to me only when viewed as a secular religion. Its main underpinning is a moral philosophy." A self-described seeker of "origins," (1987 xvii), Weisbord struggled through his definitional quest by asking colleagues, categorizing interventions, and laboring through formal definitions before arriving at his secular religious conclusion. In many respects, little has changed and reviewing his quest is as informative today as it was then. He (1977 2) wrote:

> Will anyone, I asked the literature, "define OD concisely for me, say in four paragraphs?" Said the authors:
> - It takes 5½ pages—French and Bell (1973). "…a planned, systematic process in which applied behavioral science principles and practices are introduced … a long-range effort to improve an organization's problem-solving and process" etc. etc. etc.
> - It takes 9 pages—Huse (1975) "…there exists no single definition of OD to which all practitioners would agree … the common notion underlying them all is that OD is a process for change and that OD efforts can benefit not only the organization but its numbers" etc. etc. etc.
> - It takes 13½ pages—McGill (1977) "…a conscious, planned process of developing an organization's capabilities so that it can attain and sustain an optimum level of performance as measured by efficiency, effectiveness and" etc. etc. etc.
>
> As you can see, it takes more pages every year. I scanned the chapter headings. I reviewed old *OD Practitioners*. I recalled years of OD Network meetings. OD, I discovered, has become (pick ones you like, and integrate) an interpersonal, group dynamics, TA, team-building, socio-technical, Gestalt, survey data feedback, action research, planned change, environmental, boundary management, personal style, family therapy, job enrichment, open systems, career path, female-male, black-white, performance appraisal, strategic, life planning, goal setting, conflict management, right brain, left brain, encounter, communications skills, problem solving, values clarification, bioenergetics awareness, macro systems, synergistic, creativity, MBO trip."

Classic Unifying Core Values

The confusion expressed by Weisbord between techniques and the underlying values that support those techniques is still a characteristic of some inexperienced—and, unfortunately some experienced—practitioners. The answer today, as it was nearly 50 years ago, lies in a common galvanizing set of core humanistic values. A classic early articulation of these unifying values was offered by Tannenbaum and Davis (1969 12). They viewed organization development values as … "involving movement away from older, less personally meaningful and organizationally relevant values towards these newer values." In figure 2, I have visually depicted the shift toward those "newer" values. In essence, nearly a half century ago, Tannenbaum and Davis described the foundational values of today's humanistic consulting.

Figure 2
Evolution of organization development values

FROM	TOWARD
A view of man as essentially bad ⟶	A view of man as basically good
Avoidance of negative evaluation ⟶	Evaluation that confirms people as human beings
A view of people as fixed ⟶	A view of people in process
Resistance and fear of differences ⟶	Acceptance and utilization of differences
Categorizing people according to a fixed⟶ job description	Viewing a person as a whole person
Walling off expression of feelings ⟶	Legitimizing feelings
Game playing ⟶	Authentic behavior
Irrelevant use of status ⟶	Status for organizationally relevant purposes
Distrusting people ⟶	Trusting
Avoiding facing others ⟶	Confrontation with relevant data
Avoiding risk taking ⟶	Willingness to risk
Viewing a concern over process as ⟶ unproductive	Seeing process as essential to task accomplishment
Primary emphasis on competiveness ⟶	Greater emphasis on collaboration

Organization Development as a Religion

Weisbord's notion of organization development as a secular religion was grounded in core values, not lockstep techniques that support those values. His fragmented list of techniques can be likened to individualistic practices by post-reformation Protestant denominations. A review of the contents of two contemporary organization development reference books (Rothwell, Stavros, and Sullivan 2016; Cummings and Worley 2015), reveals continuity in the diverse nature of organization development's focus and techniques. There is no one clear hierarchically dogmatic school. Much like the Protestant Reformation, organization development has, at its core, the idea that "divine revelation," in its case the process of changing and applying humanistic principals to organizations, is not the sole province of a single approach. Rather, humanistic consulting can be interpreted and implemented by a variety of people with a variety of skills at variety of organizational levels. There are, however, two fundamental characteristics of organization development practice that unify differences in application and are shared with religious tradition: coalescing statements of shared values, and continuity of core beliefs over time.

EXPLICIT ARTICULATION OF CORE BELIEFS AND VALUES

Even though they may not be able to trace their origins, responsible humanistic organization development practitioners are clear about their core values and find ways to communicate them to others. One way to view pioneers of the field such as Tannenbaum and Davis is as secular priests with a missionary zeal for their new religion, committed to not only owning their own values, but passionate about communicating and using them to change organizations. In the early years of organization development formulation, French and Bell (1973 71) stated the importance of practitioners communicating their core values and beliefs:

> One value, to which many behavioral scientists-change agents tend to give high priority, is that the needs and aspirations of human beings are the objects for organized effort in society. It is important for each behavioral scientist-change agent to make his values and beliefs visible to both himself and his client.

CONTINUITY OF CORE BELIEFS OVER TIME

Aside from a degree of erosion that will be explored in Chapter 5, the core values articulated by Tannenbaum and Davis have remarkably stood the test of time. The bedrock principles of OD—free will, belief in human potential, participation, and choice—transcend both technique, context, and level of intervention.

The similarities between organization development and religion are only useful in a metaphorical sense. OD is not a religion. It is an organizational application of humanistic principles that often results in change. Whether that change is planned or the result of an individual or organizational spontaneous "gestalt" is situational.

Values and Definitions Are Better Demonstrated Than Described: The Case of Jordan

Practitioners, particularly those early in their career, are best served to not become overly involved in definitional fine points with potential clients. As illustrated in the example of Jordan, it is far better to focus on the client's issues and let the intervention process illuminate humanistic values.

In a previous role as a line manager, I introduced Jordan, a newly minted Ph.D. who was just beginning his career as an OD practitioner, to a colleague. I knew Jordan's doctoral advisor, who gave him glowing references, so I gave Jordan a chance to build his career with a client who definitely needed help. My colleague was the newly appointed financial executive of a large computer manufacturing division. He'd inherited a dysfunctional organization of minor fiefdoms, cliques, a couple of incompetent supervisors, and lingering racial issues that resulted in a formal discrimination complaint. Although only a matchmaker, I sat through the initial—and unfortunately the last—exchange between them. Here is a paraphrased version of that interaction:

"I've got a real messy organization," said the accounting executive after the initial small talk. "They don't work as a team. They bad-mouth each other and don't seem to care about what I or their internal customers want them to do," he continued, raising to his feet and speaking with increasing intensity.

"And there is this discrimination problem that..."

"Wait, before we get into all that, I need to tell you about my values," interrupted Jordan.

"But, I want to finish telling you about..."

"No, it's important that we get clear about how I work right away," said Jordan, again interrupting. "Some practitioners see organization development as a kind of religion. I'm personally not sure but I do know that I feel called to the profession. Let me tell you why."

I began to squirm in my seat and look at the door. Jordan had a client dying to externalize his frustrations and explain his issues—a consultant's golden opportunity to learn, probe, and experience the client's needs. Rather than honor the client and respect his issues, Jordan jumped on the client's agenda with his own issues. I knew it wasn't destined to end well but to give my colleague credit, he tried again.

"We'll get to how you work and what you recommend I do, but first let me tell you what I've tried. I had an all-employee meeting last week and the woman that runs accounts payable stood up and said..."

"I use Chris Argyris' three stage intervention model—valid data, free choice, internal commitment," said Jordan, joining the client by getting to his feet and punctuating each point with a point of his finger. "Of the three, you need to understand what I mean by free choice."

And so it went. Jordan was compelled to explain his core values before he was able to hear the client's issues and form an empathetic helping relationship. The potential client grew more and more frustrated as it became clear to him that the consultant was much more interested in pursuing his agenda than that of his potential client. I was mercifully able to end the meeting after a few more futile minutes.

In a debriefing, Jordan explained that he'd learned the importance of making his values and definition of what OD stood for clear to the client. I explained that the client's needs and agenda always came first and that his humanistic values would be made clear by a collaborative, client-centered helping relationship. After a few more stumbles in other organizations, Jordan concluded that he was better suited for teaching and is now an associate professor of organizational behavior at a state university.

There are three lessons from Jordan's short-lived consulting career. The first is that the client's needs always come first. In the case of incompatible values, the consultant can simply walk away, but first she has an obligation to work to understand the client. The second lesson is that humanistic values are better demonstrated than explained. The final learning is that even though, as aptly described in the title of Bellman's (2002) book, *The Consultant's Calling*, if the practitioner feels irresistibly drawn to the profession, clients are much more interested in solving their own problems than hearing about the consultant's motivation.

Advice and Recommendations

- For both the researcher and the practitioner seeking to discover the eclectic, boundary-spanning dimensions of the early years of organization development, it is strongly recommended that you obtain a copy of Bennis, Benne and Chin's (1961), *The Planning of Change*. Be sure to find the 1961 edition. Subsequent editions have reduced the size and eliminated some contributors. It may take some searching to find a copy, but only in the 1961 edition will you find a depiction of the widespread academic and practitioner heterogeneity of the times.

- If you are an organization development consultant, chances are you struggle to explain exactly what you do. Many successful OD consultants don't use the term organization development at all. They focus on telling clients that they help develop teams, improve group processes, collaborate to facilitate change that will help improve productivity and the quality of work-life. They explain that they help leaders get clearer insights into the effect of their behavior on others.

- Because of its grounding in humanistic values, some practitioners, like Bellman, see themselves as "called" to the field and some are comfortable with the religious connotation. If you are one, it is best to keep the religious metaphor to yourself. Clients want to be helped, not converted, and labeling what you do as practicing a secular religion is guaranteed to scare clients away.

- If you are seeking help don't be put off by consultant marginality. If consultants thought, acted, and saw issues the same as you, they wouldn't be of much value. On the other hand, if one insists on imposing her values on you, negatively judges your behavior, doesn't give you free choice, and can't find common ground, get rid of her. She's not an OD consultant, she is an irresponsible evangelist, much more interested in her agenda than yours.

- If you are an organization development practitioner, your power and effectiveness depend on your ability to translate your values into your client's frame of reference. It's important to be clear and explicit concerning your values, but, OD pioneer and founder of the Pepperdine OD Master's program, Pat Williams, emphasized a simple but profound guideline to his students: "Meet the client where the client is, not where you want him to be."

3. The Beginning: Three Wise Men and the Birth of NTL

"I was never satisfied with the ideas or idea systems
which were not somehow oriented to the needs
of action in the society."—*Kenneth Benne*

Martin Luther's nailing of his thesis on the door of the Castle Church in Wittenberg in 1517 was the historical start of the Protestant Reformation. In 1947, a similar beginning took place in organization development. This time the door was that of the gymnasium of Gould Academy and the location was Bethel, Maine. The three people wielding the hammer in protestation of the prevailing views of "scientific management" were Lee Bradford, Ron Lippitt, and Ken Benne.

I made a pilgrimage to Bethel in the late 1980s. My first impression was that the Mecca of organization development had become more like a commercial conference center. However, with a little effort, it was easy to fantasize and commune with the ghosts of the founding fathers. Sometimes they were present in the flesh. Both Bob Tannenbaum and Ron Lippitt were in residence that week.

Something profound and meaningful unfolded during those early years in Bethel and it's easy in today's world of techniques and gimmicks, to underestimate the spiritual power that came together in 1947. The times (post–World War II), the influence of people like Douglas McGregor and Kurt Lewin, the sense of mission and shared values of Benne, Lippitt, and Bradford, all coalesced and formed the values and humanistic mission of what today we call organization development.

The Birth of National Training Labs

Aside from the ambience, T-group experience, and the opportunity to commune with the ghosts of the field, a tangible outcome of that visit many years ago was the acquisition of the book, *National Training Laboratories, Its History: 1947–1970* (Bradford, 1974). This publication is a significant resource for those interested in examining the philosophical and value influences on the beginnings of humanistic practice. It not only includes source documents such as outlines and process comments on early labs, but also features an introduction by each of the three founders. These introductions explain the educational, social, and humanistic influences that not only led to the formation of the National Training Labs (NTL), but also formed the foundation for the practice of OD. It is an exceptional historical treasure that ought to be required reading in organization development graduate programs.

THE INFLUENCE OF KURT LEWIN AND DOUGLAS MCGREGOR

Even through Lewin died shortly before the first NTL session in the summer of 1947, he was the spiritual and intellectual founder. He was responsible for starting what is now known as "action research," coined the term "group dynamics," and was a pioneer in applying the concept of "normative, re-educative" change. His notion of force field analysis provided a conceptual framework for facilitating change. Lewin's focus was on using humanistic ideas to solve social problems through groups, a unique departure from academic psychology's orientation at the time. Weisbord (1987 96) describes this perspective:

> By 1954 Kurt Lewin had determined to use social science to alter systems, not just to describe them. He saw changing individual behavior as a weak, even futile strategy for intractable social problems. Productive workplaces were a community responsibility. From his wartime experiments, he concluded that managing participation required skilled leadership. Someone had to fertilize the soil for effective groups to take root. Developing such group leaders called for an applied social science far outside academic psychology.

Douglas McGregor, at the time a professor of psychology at MIT, saw in Lewin's research and interests, a way to create win/win outcomes to polarizing labor relations issues. With McGregor's assistance, Lewin started the Research Center for Group Dynamics at MIT. This center, which later moved to the University of Michigan, had an outside-the-traditional-academic-box focus on training leaders in group process and facilitating change.

In 1946, Lewin brought the three wise men together in response to a request from Connecticut's Inter-Racial Commission's request for training sessions to help leaders deal with religious and racial prejudice. It was in these sessions that the seeds of NTL were planted and the power of feedback, process observation, participation, and the T-group were discovered. Kurt Lewin died in in 1947 but the approach forged in the Connecticut workshops was carried forward in Bethel by Benne, Bradford, and Lippitt.

The reason Bethel, Maine, became the early Mecca of group dynamics and the cradle of organization development was because of a grant obtained by Lewin from the Office of Naval Research to run summer workshops in a boarding school there. Why Bethel? "It was a cultural island (translation: small town, hard to reach). Picked because it was thought people would unfreeze faster outside the office" (Weisbord 1987, 101).

Humanistic Foundations of Three Wise Men

A brief review of the self-described interests and values of the three founders provides insight into the energy and passion they brought to Bethel.

Ron Lippitt. Lippitt graduated from Springfield College in 1936 and was already involved in group process work with the YMCA. He did his graduate studies at Iowa under Kurt Lewin. His early research included a classic autocracy-democracy study on learning. Lewin brought him to Washington to take his place in the OSS assessment center toward the end of World War II. Lippitt succinctly describes his interests and contribution (Bradford 1974 13): "Thus, in many ways my training and experience formed one of the components that led us to form the National Training Laboratory. I brought not only research knowledge and skill, but also an abiding interest in application of research knowledge in action."

Kenneth Benne. Benne was interested in applied social psychology and the philosophy of education. He taught a "Philosophy and Social Foundations of Education" course at the University of Illinois in 1941. Just as Lippitt was interested in action research, Benne was interested in education for social change—another deep root of organization development and connection to humanism. He says in his introduction (Bradford 1974 14):

I think I should also note another stream in my development which fed into my interest in the laboratory methods of education.... I had brought with me from Kansas a somewhat radical orientation to social affairs ... this means that I was never satisfied with the ideas or idea systems which were not somehow oriented to the needs of action in the society.... I had a strong career bias for a life in education, and I suppose I could reconcile this career commitment with my concern for action and interest in social improvement with an education that was designed to train men for democratic action.

Leland Bradford. Bradford seemed more interested in the practical hands-on adult education process. The following (Bradford 1974 23) provides an example of the forces driving him as far back as 1928:

In 1928 I returned to the university through the help of the father of a friend I was tutoring. I managed to squeeze out a degree in 1930. I knew then that I wanted to teach properly but the depression was on and few jobs were available so I returned to work on tabulating machines in a mail order house. It wasn't long before I became aware of the cultural starvation of my fellow employees and I felt it my duty to do something about it. Starting with one student, I gradually introduced a dozen persons to spend three nights a week in what I called "The Bradford Academy."

The forces that drove these early pioneers gave birth to the energy and uniqueness that sustains and differentiates the best of today's humanistic consultants. Throughout the depression years and into the early years of World War II, the three of them were committed to broad-based social change. They wanted this change to enrich people's lives and make the world a better place. In 1932, Lippitt worked with process analysis for impoverished children through the YMCA. In 1928, Lee Bradford was teaching a free adult education clinic in a dilapidated building on the north side of Chicago, and Kenneth Benne was utilizing sub-groups and discussion methods in his teaching at the University of Illinois in 1941.

Based their experiences and interests, these NTL founders stood on a three-legged stool when they nailed their thesis on the door of the Gould Academy in 1947. The first leg was their collective experience in normative, re-educative change forged through their work with the National Education Association, federal agencies, and university affiliations. The second leg was their shared beliefs and values that adult education could be used to facilitate human understanding and lead to the elimination of war. The third leg was funding from federal, state, and private foundations to allow them to study change processes.

An Under-Appreciated Mecca

It is an unfortunate reality that many of today's OD practitioners know so little of the roots of their discipline and the seminal contributions of Bradford, Lippitt, and Benne. It is even more unfortunate that the contribution of the National Training Laboratories is glossed over and not covered at all in some graduate OD programs. For the serious student of the application of humanistic values to organizational consultation there is no better place to begin than the lives and values of the three wise men who founded the National Training Labs. Although NTL has significantly evolved from the early days and the NTL institute is now headquartered in Silver Spring, Maryland, it remains a cultural repository of the founder's core values of inclusion, collaboration, and social change. Bethel, Maine, was no Mecca and there was no requirement for practitioners to undertake a pilgrimage, but, back in the day, a visit to the secluded woods of Maine and the accompanying appreciation of the historical roots of organization development practice was a very effective antidote to humanistic consultant burnout and idealistic jading.

Advice and Recommendations

- The three wise men, Lippitt, Benne, and Bradford, under the guidance of the fourth, and perhaps the wisest of the wise—Kurt Lewin—planted the seeds of what we today know as organization development in the backwoods of Maine. Those seeds were nourished by a belief in humanistic values and normative, re-educative change as a mechanism to promote equality, enhance participation and thereby change the world and end war—no small goal.

- If you are a practitioner, take the time and expend the energy to learn the early history of your field. Start by reading Bradford's (1974) *National Training Laboratories, Its History: 1947–1970*. If at all possible, attend an NTL program.

- If you are a line manager, know that your life will be enhanced and you will be a much more effective leader by attending a T-group. As long as it is led by competent facilitators, it certainly doesn't need to be offered by NTL. However, NTL events are not the exclusive territory of humanistic consultants. All are welcome.

- If you are involved in teaching and research at the either the graduate or undergraduate level, don't overlook the seminal role of NTL's founders. They gave birth to humanistic organizational intervention and you can't teach or research OD without beginning with them.

4. The Formative Years: Outsiders, Stems, Roots and Streams

"The clinicians who came had little orientation to social action or broader social change."—*Lee Bradford*

A revealing transition occurred in Bethel's third year, 1949. It stimulated the debate over the focus on personal growth as opposed to the development of change agents capable of transforming organizations and changing society. This was the year that "outsiders" made their influence known at NTL and the founding fathers began to see their flock fragment. Bradford (1974 20–21) describes this period:

> In many ways I found that in 1949, a kind of watershed year both in my relationships with NTL, and perhaps in the overall development of NTL as an organization. The laboratory staff brought in a large number of clinically oriented staff members. These were of both Rogerian and Freudian persuasion ... people who had not shared in any significant way the deliberations, the collaborations, the thinking of Lee, Ron, myself, and others who had been incorporated into the core staff during its first two years of operation. Qualitatively the influx also represented a felt need for people more clinically oriented both from psychiatry and from clinical psychology. The effect ... was to push Lee, Ron, and myself from a central position in laboratory affairs.

Bradford described his "resistance" to the influx of newcomers as partially a reaction to the process of "dethronement." He, however, also described his alienation as a reaction to the focus of the new arrivals on individual change and development. He continues, (p. 21):

> But, partially, also, I think I objected to the rather partial interpretations which newcomers put upon the enterprise. I have already made it clear that I saw it as part of a process of social action. The clinicians who came had little orientation to social action or broader social change. Their training and background tended to lead them to focus upon changes in personal and interpersonal relations ... my battles of 1949 were probably, therefore, based on some feeling of being

pushed over to a more peripheral position within the scheme of NTL; but I think they equally reflected concerns growing out of my social radicalism which I have mentioned earlier and which I saw as being served by NTL as I had seen it developing within the larger society and culture.

A Positive Influx

Although Bradford had reservations concerning the "newcomers," their passion and contributions substantially shaped the fields of organization development and organizational behavior.

Bradford's "influx" of new people into the research and training staff reads like a hall of fame for both organizational behavior luminaries and organization development practitioners. In 1948 Ron Lippitt's brother, Gordon, came to a lab for the first time. In 1950 an advisory committee was set up. Two of the more notable members were Rensis Likert and Douglas McGregor. Chris Argyris was a resident member of the research staff during this year. Many of the early staff members were, in their own way, founders of various sects of organization development. Among the names listed in the research and training staff during the 1950s were Richard Beckhard, Jack Gibb, Fritz Roethlisberger, Robert Blake, Charles Seashore, Ed Schein, and Herb Shepard. In 1960 Jerry Harvey appeared on a list of "interns serving as co-trainers."

In the 1947 through 1960 time frame, "outsiders" helped shape some fundamental building blocks of organization development practice. T-groups, process observation, the developmental stages of a learning community, and "here-and-now." action research were refined and developed.

The Lab of Laboratory Training: The T-Group

Although NTL wasn't the sole tap root into humanistic values that nurtured the birth of organization development, it was certainly the primary contributor, and central to the development of NTL was the training group (T-group). The birth of the training group can be traced to a 1946 race relations training program conducted by Kurt Lewin that included Lee Bradford, Ron Lippitt, and Kenneth Benne. By accident, the trainers and researchers found that after-hours discussions and impression sharing with participants resulted in enhanced "here-and now" learning for both participants and staff to the extent that this unstructured interaction was much more productive than the formal program and became the essence of the training itself. (Weisbord 1987 100).

Central to the T-group experience is the use of an unstructured group experience to deepen one's understanding of the impact of one's behavior on group process; discover "in-the-moment" insights as to how others' behavior impacts one's self-perception and behavior; learn the power of skillfully giving and receiving feedback; differentiate between judgmental and descriptive behavior; and productively deal with feelings and emotions (Seashore 1999). Learnings from T-groups can be applied to individual development, more authentic and productive group process, and, of course, humanistically focused organization development interventions.

The term evolved into "sensitivity training" in the 1960s, and because of untrained and sometimes manipulative facilitators, it developed a bad reputation among some managers and organization development practitioners. Nonetheless, the T-group experience, under the guidance of a competent facilitator, is seen by many development professionals as their single most powerful learning experience. Referencing a session at the Academy of Management, Minahan and Crosby (2016 362) write:

> It was at the Academy of Management annual conference in 2009 in Chicago that many of the past chairs of the OD Division of the Academy—including Stafford Beer, Warner Burke, Frank Friedlander, Larry Greiner, Bob Golembiewski, Craig Lundberg, and Dale Zand among others, cited their T-group experience as the moment that changed their lives for the better. These leaders in leadership, management, and OD said it was in their T-group experiences and training that they learned to notice process, to operate in the here and now, to test their observations and inferences before acting, and to empathize with others in ways that had not happened previously.

Vaill (1985 558) reacts to the belief among some that "sensitivity training" was "the stuff of parity ... basically just one more nutty idea from the sixties," with an unqualified affirmation. "I think that sensitivity training is the most original and powerful contribution that the applied behavioral sciences have made to civilized culture." What prompted this endorsement was Vaill's belief that a genuine T-group experience relied on the value of "trusting the process."

Origin of the Name "Organization Development"

The term, organization development, was coined during the new person "influx"—most likely in the late 1950s—to differentiate a past focus on the individual, "individual development," to a focus on the organization, "organization development." The exact date and credit for the term is not clear. Porter (1974 1) credits both Dick Beckhard while consulting with General Electric and Herb Shepard while working with Esso. Both consultations took place in 1957. In an interview with Marshall Shaskin (1981 20), Gordon Lippitt said, "Alfred Morrow said he heard Kurt Lewin use the word in his basement for the first time. Bob Blake and Jane Mouton said they used it the first time on their way to the Esso Bay refinery. Of course, Dick Beckhard and I will say that we used it for the first time in our work with the Red Cross."

A bit of trivia for the declining number of organization development practitioners still wedded to the use of newsprint flip charts in their work: Bradford (1974) credits Ron Lippitt, working at Friedman's Hospital in 1946, as the first to use newsprint in training work. According to Weisbord (1976), the practice was a derivative of Kurt Lewin's habit of drawing force fields on butcher paper taped to a wall in the 1946 Connecticut Inter-Racial Workshops.

Stems, Roots and Streams

The Survey Feedback Process

Huse (1975 24) gives credit to Kurt Lewin for developing the process of survey feedback where data is fed back to a group and they process and deal with the information. He adds it to the T-group as one of the two "stems" of organization development: "OD comes from two related but different stems. The first is the growth of the National Training Laboratories and the development of training groups. The second basic stem comes from the early work in survey research and feedback."

Kurt Lewin was instrumental in the development of both stems and was also an important influence in encouraging groups to process their own data. He founded the Research Center for Group Dynamics in 1945. After he died in 1947, his staff moved to Michigan to join the Survey Research Center which became the Institute for Social Research.

The Tavistock Institute

The London-based Tavistock Institute contributed in two areas: a practical understanding of group dynamics and the evolution of what are now called socio-technical systems. Examples of Tavistock's influence on theories of group behavior, group therapy, and connection to group humanistic consultation can be found in Wilfred Bion's *Experience in Groups* (1961). The influence of this orientation is reflected in Douglas McGregor's description of an early Tavistock training design (Bennis, Benne and Chin 1961 621): "Douglas McGregor has informed us that Tavistock Institute has been tackling their problem in a rather different and creative way. Before the actual training design begins, the training staff spends some time with the trainee at the work place and then tries to diagnose work-relevant problems that ultimately are used as a basis for the training design." Collaborating with participants, jointly diagnosing issues, and partnering in training design, may seem like old hat today but it was revolutionary in the late fifties.

An important root of the Tavistock influence was the work of Trist and Bamforth on the effects of a change in technology on productivity. In a well-documented case study in a South Yorkshire coal mine, the shift from an older (long wall), fragmented method of production to a new process where miners were multi-skilled and performed all tasks, produced a significant increase in productivity. This and similar studies in a textile firm in India highlighted the importance of "socio-tech" interventions: connecting the dynamics of the work group to technology. Trist's reaction and the OD implications are explained by Scherer, Alban and Weisbord (2016 31):

> He realized the connection between England's business recovery and what he had just seen, putting together the therapeutic work Bion and he had done with shared leadership in groups and Lewin's work in small group dynamics. If given the proper supports and resources, Trist hypothesized, teams could redesign how they plan, manage, and do their work—and produce at higher levels. Because of our 50 years of OD hindsight, it is hard for us to realize the dynamic impact of this discovery!

In an earlier work (1983 3), Weisbord talks of streams, not roots or stems: "One stream began after World War II in the coal mines of Northwest Durham in the United Kingdom. There a group from Tavistock Institute ... began to investigate the connections between the division of labor, the equipment, and the social systems of the coal miners."

To this stream, he added another: the influence of Lewin and the birth of NTL. His third stream is the use of survey feedback where he credits Floyd Mann and others at the University of Michigan's Institute for Social Research. For his fourth stream, which is essentially part of the

NTL stream, he gives recognition to Chris Argyris when he writes, "If we add to these, Chris Argyris's powerful theory of intervention—valid data, free choice, commitment to act—which was an outgrowth of the T-group movement, I think we have the major foundations of current OD practice."

Two Foundational Theories

Regardless of the visualization—roots, stems, or streams—a foundation is necessary to provide the rocks over which the streams flow and the soil that nourishes the roots and stems. Maslow's needs theory and McGregor's theory of motivational assumptions provided this foundation.

Maslow's theory provided a philosophical counterpoint to the scientific management—man is a machine—viewpoint of the time. Machines don't strive for self-actualization and people do. Maslow developed his needs theory in 1943. Seventeen years later with the immensely popular publication of *The Human Side of Enterprise* (1960), McGregor caused leaders to consider and evaluate contrasting assumptions concerning human motivation. Some researchers either relegate McGregor's theories X and Y to trivia or dispute its science. It was, however, as Peter Vaill wrote (2009 19) "...arguably the most influential book of the last fifty years in terms of presenting the case for 'the human side of enterprise.'"

Figure 3 is a summary of the contributions of those who influenced the theory and evolution of organization development.

Advice and Recommendations

- Looking at what Bradford described as an influx of outsiders in 1947 from the perspective of seventy years, it would appear that these "new" voices provided a needed focus and reality check on his self-described "social radicalism." Not that social radicalism is incompatible with humanism, but the "outsiders" hooked humanistic interventions to real, ongoing organizations and provided practical boundaries on radicalism. Survey feedback, sociotechnical approaches, and small group process consultation, were imported by "outsiders" and helped NTL and the organization

Figure 3
Contributors to the evolution of organization development

CONTRIBUTORS	IMPACT	OUTCOMES
Abraham Maslow	Needs theory	Self-Actualization, Personal growth, Foundational intervention theory
Douglas McGregor	Motivational theory	Examination & awareness of motivational assumptions
Kurt Lewin	Primary influencer to NTL founders	Survey-feedback Force field analysis Action research
NTL Founders: Benne, Bradford & Chinn	Education for social action	Normative, re-educative change T-groups Institutionalized laboratory training and research
Influx of "new" NTL Faculty	Refinement & expansion of concepts and interventions	T-groups Process observation Developmental Stages of a learning communities Action research
Tavistock Institute: Trist, Bamforth & Bion	Group dynamics	Socio-Tech awareness & interventions Group behavioral theory
Chris Argyris	Intervention theory	Valid data-free choice-internal commitment methodology

development movement grow and not put all their eggs in the radical social change basket. The organization transformation movement of the mid–1980s described in Chapter 7 was essentially a re-orientation of some OD practitioners to the social change agenda of Bradford, Benne, and Lippitt.

- If you are an OD practitioner or an operating manager attempting to function in a humanistic consulting style without experiencing a T-group, you'll not only be missing a lot of arrows in your consulting quiver, you'll be robbing yourself of significant intrapersonal insight, process savvy, and interpersonal competence. If you're doing any form of humanistic consulting, find a way to participate in a T-group. Make sure it's under the guidance of a competent facilitator. NTL's human interaction labs are one option and there are many others. Don't miss the opportunity for the necessary personal growth. To excel in organization development you need to experience a T-group.

39

- Although old, Maslow's (1943) and McGregor's (1960) theories provide important groundwork for today's practitioner. It is worth dusting off old textbooks or looking up references to become reacquainted with these foundational theories. I have also found it a very helpful bonding experience to share these theories with clients.

5. The OD Practitioner

"...the practitioner may be the only person
able to take a risk, to confront, to ask
the fool's hard questions."—*Larry Porter*

When an experienced organization development practitioner was asked to explain her involvement in a large business organization she simply said, "I'm doin' some stuff in one of their divisions." Whether in respect for client confidentiality or with an awareness that an accurate answer would be too long and detailed for the occasion, the questioner just nodded his head and changed the subject.

That "stuff" she was doing required a lot of courage. Porter (1978 5) said it this way: "In such a setting the practitioner may be the only person to take a risk, to confront, to ask the fool's hard questions. And in our practice, we must constantly do these things."

Her answer was clear in another dimension: organization development consultants *do* things in organizational settings. They *practice* OD. The journal of the National OD Network is called the *OD Practitioner*. The practitioner intervenes in a client system with the purpose of generating valid data, giving the client free choice about what to do with it, and helping, should the client choose to change. These are the classic tasks of the interventionist as described by Argyris (1973).

Today's practitioner has a staggering array of diagnostic and intervention options. A comprehensive, contemporary organization development textbook (Cummings and Worley 2015) outlines three possible levels of diagnosis (organizational, group, and individual) and for each level, multiple tools and analytical techniques are available. Intervention choices include human process, technostructural, human resource, and strategic change. Each type of intervention, in turn, has many optional techniques and sub-processes. With such a complex maze of diagnostic and intervention options and the constant threat of burn-out and cynicism, the wise practitioner seeks peer consultation, feedback, and often partners with others in his practice. Even with the best assistance, in order to remain relevant, the consultant must work hard to avoid the many hazards that lurk in the shadows of his practice.

Threats to Practitioner Authenticity and Effectiveness

BECOMING A SOLUTION LOOKING FOR A PROBLEM

Practitioners wedded to a favorite diagnostic process or instrument such as a form of survey-feedback, a 360-degree assessment process or an instrument such as the Meyers-Briggs Type Indicator, can slip into a pattern that may serve their preferences rather than their client's needs. Likewise, practitioners favoring an intervention such as team building or process consultation, can overlook techniques and levels of intervention that may be of better use to their clients.

BURNING OUT AND FAILURE TO NURTURE THEIR OWN VALUES AND SKILLS

This danger is as alive and well today as it was when Porter articulated it in an early article in the *OD Practitioner* (Porter 1978) with the intriguing title "OD Practice: Some Extrapolations, Metaphors, and Inferential Leaps." The article was part of Porter's speech to the opening session of the Academy of Management's OD Division. Here is an excerpt (p. 2):

> Practice, on the other hand is all over the map—and so are practitioners. Practice is pragmatic, reward-seeking, skewed by certain organizational realities, value-laden, sloppy, murky, sometimes more dependent on who's practicing than on particular theories espoused. Practitioners do reach out for things that work, they do smirgle up what it is they're doing (often defined by "Is it helping the client?" rather than "Is it OD?"); they also get lonely and burned-out, and sometimes in dealing with those factors they stumble onto solutions which they attempt to draw back into their work. But many of us have come into the field through National Training Laboratories, and that organization does not have a reputation for uptightness and rigidity. So here we are, while not exactly a beads-and-incense gang, very much concerned, not only with learning theory and organization behavior concepts, but what might be called some of the "fringier" manifestations of the behavioral sciences. Among OD practitioners, then, there is great interest in activities and theories related to themselves as people—people

who use themselves as tools and thus have a tendency to grow rusty, blunt (or over-sharp), or burn-out. Most practitioners I know do see themselves in their work with clients—theories and activities related to self-replenishment, re-creation, and self-nurturance.

Erosion of Necessary Marginality

One definition of a marginal person (Cummings and Worley 2015 54) is: "...one who successfully straddles the boundary between two or more groups with differing goals, value systems and behavior patterns." The basic concept of consultant marginality is that the consultant should be different enough from her client to add value. In traditional management consulting it means that the consultant has a skill set or technical knowledge that allows her to prescribe solutions to the client. In organization development consulting, marginality requires process skills, interpersonal competence, intra-personal awareness, systems thinking, helping skills, and humanistic values, that, in combination, are different or more developed than the line manager.

Declining legacy of the 1960s. The 1960s were the zenith of what was labeled "the human potential movement," a countercultural mix of groups that believed that the key to happy, creative lives involved accessing a reservoir of untapped potential within each person. The concept was a derivative of humanistic psychology and influenced by Abraham Maslow's theory of self-actualization. The values of openness, participation, and free will were congruent with those of humanism. Although gaining a degree of legitimacy through affiliation with the Esalen Institute, the movement became associated with psychedelic culture and cult-like groups such as "EST" and "Life Spring."

Many practitioners in the 1960s were strongly influenced by the core tenets of the human potential movement. There was a connection between the way they viewed organizations—particularly those of the large, for-profit variety—and their humanistic values. They were attracted to organization development because of their mistrust of large, bureaucratic organizations. They wanted to make them more open, democratic, participative, and diverse. These objectives were often in contrast to those of clients who had difficulty connecting these values to the making of money and their prevailing hierarchical organizational cultures. It was a win/win relationship when the consultant was able to honor the client's values without compromising his own and when the client was able to grasp the fact that enhanced self-awareness, better group process and employee involvement would, not only lead to greater profits, but a sustainable enriched work environment.

In many of today's quarter-to-quarter, numbers-only oriented organizations, short term-bottom line mania has devalued the power of marginality. The 1960s are long gone and so is organizational tolerance for overly marginal consultants and, too often, respect for their humanistic principles. There appears to be an increasing number of consultants who purport to be practicing organization development who are not only unfamiliar with the core humanistic values of the profession, but don't possess the requisite interpersonal competence, intra-personal awareness, and fundamental process skills. They are essentially traditional management consultants, operating under an OD label.

FOUNDATIONAL DECAY AND WITHERED ROOTS

In 2016 postings on two LinkedIn social network sites, one made up of approximately 40,000 members with an interest in organization development and the other, an HR group of about 975,000 members, resulted in some interesting responses. I asked why many HR professionals didn't know what OD stood for. The question was posed in regard to the underlying conceptual values but some respondents thought the question was what the letters stood for and a surprising number didn't seem to know. One respondent thought they stood for "oppositional defiance," several thought they represented "organizational design," and a few just stated they didn't know and asked for clarification. Some—hopefully intending humor—commented that OD dealt with overdosing, olive drab (a designation for the color of Army uniforms), or that the letter "C" was missing from OCD. Of the responses from those who knew the meaning of the term, most saw organization development only as a means to increase profits and return on investment. Not that these aren't essential to for-profit organizations, but to the practitioner grounded in humanistic values, so are the quality of work-life, human potential, inclusiveness, and participation.

According to some researchers (Worley and Feyerherm 2003 97) there has been an erosion of the core organization development values which had long been the professional standard and are depicted in figure two:

> In the early 1990s, Warner Burk and Allen Church examined these values ... and
> compared value lists generated by Bennis, Beckhard, and Tannenbaum with their

own list. There were some obvious differences. In particular, Church, Burk, and Van Eynde (1994) noted that the practice of OD had become more "results" and "bottom-line" oriented. The expression of personal power and reaping the rewards of consulting relationships had become the most prominent motivators in practitioners' current modes of operation.

The long-held belief that it is necessary for practitioners to take a time-out from practice for self-renewal also seems under question. In interviews of "21 thought leaders and pioneers in the field of OD," Worley and Feyerham (2003) found a split between those who saw the primary consultant focus on self-development such as T-groups, and those who discounted the value. They write (p. 108): "One side of the fault line sees self-development as the sine qua non of OD, whereas the other side argues its irrelevance in practice and theory."

Jamieson and Rothwell (2016 387) describe a move toward organizational efficiency: "OD operates mostly at the whole organization systems level (including sub-units of larger wholes). It pursues organizational effectiveness by working on all parts of the socio-technical system that makes up any organization. It was always best known for its focus on the human element, but that is not all that is important."

The danger is that as OD becomes more and more involved in whole system redesign, strategies, and structure it will become less and less grounded in foundational humanistic values, lose its differentiation and morph into traditional management consulting. Jamieson and Rothwell (2016 387) outline the necessary balance when they conceptualize OD as, "a process of planned intervention(s) utilizing behavioral and organizational science principles to change a system and improve its effectiveness, *conducted in accordance with values of humanism, participation, choice, and development so the organization and its members learn and develop*" (emphasis added).

Developing and Partnering with "Practitioner" Line Managers

Organization development practitioners have traditionally been exporters, bringing their skills, interventions, and marginal perspectives into existing organizational systems. Line (operational) managers have traditionally been importers, retaining humanistic consultants from outside their corporations to help increase productivity, facilitate change, and enhance the quality of work life. Even when managers contract with internal organization development consultants, the practitioners represent a different culture.

The complexity of organizations requires a hybrid model. While operational managers must be focused on the so called "hard side," (profits, marketing, production, and strategy), there is nothing that prevents them from acquiring proficiency in the pejoratively labeled "soft side," which in reality is at least equally hard. There will always be a need for specialized, marginal, OD practitioners to mentor operational managers but the process can be much more collegial than in the past. To be truly effective in today's complex, global organizational systems, operational managers need personal proficiency in group process facilitation and team building. They need a high degree of interpersonal competence and humanistic grounding to effectively relate to the modern workforce. The challenge for the OD practitioner is to help develop operational managers with the requisite humanistic and diagnostic skills. The challenge for the manager is to embrace the "soft side," for it will make them much more relevant leaders.

An occurrence at a past organization development conference will illustrate that there is some distance to go to accomplish this integration. A general manager of a division of an international corporation who also had a Ph.D. in clinical psychology and had been operating in a hybrid mode, partnering with external consultants and jointly facilitating humanistic interventions for nearly twenty years, accompanied me to an OD convention. The name tags of those attending had a space designating the number of years the wearer had "been in OD." Since the manager had always "been in" management but also practiced OD, and wanted to make a point, he coded his badge with a "0." In the elevator he ran into a colleague who had a "5" displayed on her nametag. The executive told her he was a line manager, but utilized OD concepts in the way he managed. She asked, "Who does your OD?" He said, "I do," and received a supercilious smile and another question. "Do you have an OD department?" He said his whole organization was an OD department. The elevator then stopped and she got off, no doubt anxious to tell her friends about the strange "line guy" she had met. We were left wondering how many other practitioners wanted to do OD *to* line management and not *with* them.

46

Partnering with HR Professionals

The relationship of internal OD practitioners and the human resource function has long been a subject of debate. In some organizations the differences extend to the retention of outside consultants, with HR claiming responsibility for screening and hiring external OD consultants, and line managers along with internal practitioners wanting to bypass HR and do it on their own.

For internal practitioners a central issue is their reporting relationship. Human resource functions claim responsibility for the development and nurturing of both individuals and organizational systems. After all, they say, the component of these activities is "human resources," and, thus, feel that the OD function ought to report to the function that bears that name. Internal organization development practitioners argue for a reporting relationship outside of the human resource function—usually to the CEO or someone in top management. Their rationale is that HR is too invested in administration and control to foster the objectivity and freedom necessary for authentic organization development.

Jamieson and Rothwell (2016 389) get at the central issue when they discuss the Yin and Yang of human resource management:

> HRM has historically been conflicted, with one half focused on organizational compliance with government laws, rules, regulations, organizational policies and procedures and collective bargain agreements where they may exist. That half, the yin of HRM, is defensive (as in sports) in the sense of preventing loss and minimizing risks. The other half of HRM, the yang, is offensive (also as in sports) and should maximize productivity, human performance, creativity and innovation. OD is more in alignment with the yang part, such that OD is an offensive issue. OD creates and sustains organizational cultures in which the human spirit can flourish, creative and innovative thought can be maximize, and human productivity can be enhanced.

Just as operational managers can incorporate humanistic organization development values and techniques into their roles, so can human resource professionals—not just those in the more naturally fitting "Yang" roles, but also those on the "Yin" side of the human resource equation. Whether it reports inside or outside the human resource function, organization development should be independent and operate autonomously. Regardless of whether organization development is part of the HR structure, the credibility and contribution of all HR functions can be greatly enhanced by acquiring the basic OD skills of non-evaluative listening, knowing how to give and receive feedback in ways that are helpful and constructive, a basic knowledge of the consequences of making people defensive, and an understanding the impact of their own agenda on any situation.

The Guru Phenomenon

There are some practitioners who have achieved guru-like standing. Some have achieved national status and others are revered inside individual organizations, sometimes only in sub-organizational units. Vaill (1985 569) frames the process of achieving guru status on the dynamics of authenticity, active listing, genuinely caring about the client, not relying on external technique, and being who you are as a person. "The best active listeners care about the person they are trying to listen to ... what is to be learned from them is not 'how they do it,' but how they are as persons."

A number of years ago, I was walking back from a practitioner training session with another participant when she asked, "Why is it that I follow Art Shedlund around like a little puppy dog, hanging on his every word and instructor 'X' has no effect on me whatsoever?" More recently, an external consultant sought advice. "They seemed to like what I did and learned a lot in that team building session," she said, referring to a group of mangers in a high technology company. "There's more work to be done but I can't understand why they didn't want me back, but consultant 'Y' waltzed in after me and they love him, put him on retainer and are doing lots of 'stuff' with him. Why not me?"

THE POWER OF AUTHENTICITY

What was it that made Art Shedlund so different for that participant? What caused those managers to roll out the red carpet for one consultant and reject another? What made someone like Bob Tannenbaum create an impact far beyond his actual words and message? The answer, as Vaill states, lies in these practitioners being who they are, and responding to clients in a unique one-time phenomenological frame. The organization development field is filled with an amazing array of intervention techniques and diagnostic processes but most practitioners who have been involved for any length of time can trace their own personal development to interactions with one or two significant people. It is these people, being who they are, not their tools or techniques that make the difference. I have seen very hard core, cynical managers, changed by a meaningful interaction with a practitioner. They didn't know exactly what transpired, only that she or he, "listened to me," "talked to me," and "made a difference to me."

The most relevant tool is the practitioner's warm body. The humanistic consultant who is open, behaves congruently with his values, and is able to caringly confront both colleagues and clients, is much more powerful than any diagnostic instrument or process intervention. When working at his best, the greatest practitioner's tool is his own warm body. I have been on both sides of the table: practitioner and client. My best practitioner work has been when I spontaneously and interactively worked with the client without relying on techniques or gimmicks. When I've been a client, I have also been moved and touched by authentic, non–gimmick-based interactions. It's not easy to achieve this authenticity because one has to set aside preconditioned assumptions and experience each interaction as a unique event. What philosophers (Buckingham et al. 2011 224) describe as a unique phenomenological occurrence.

There have always been gurus with the ability to create deep phenomenological connections: Jesus, Siddhartha Gautama (the historic Buddha), Confucius, Gandhi, and Martin Luther King are examples. Humanistic practitioners don't aspire to operate at those levels of spiritual connection. Despite the somewhat arrogant use of the term applied behavioral *science*, organization development consultants deal with the linkage between individuals and organizations, applying their "guruism" intuitively, not scientifically, to the facilitation of organizational change.

All organization development practitioners acting in accord with humanistic values who are not seduced by over-reliance on technique are gurus, only the scope of their influence varies. The utilization of the practitioner him or herself as the primary instrument of change and the concurrent lack of reliance on techniques, is what some senior practitioners mean when they express a desire to "go back to the way it was."

Advice and Recommendations

- Larry Porter's timeless comment that the OD practitioner may be the only person "who is able to take a risk, to confront, to ask the fool's hard questions" cogently captures the power of the practitioner's marginality.
- To survive and remain relevant, practitioners need to resist the pervasive threats to the essence of their effectiveness: their marginality.

Becoming a solution seeking a problem (over reliance on one technique or intervention process); the threat of burn-out and failure to nurture and develop the primary intervention tool (their own warm body); and the economic and status seduction of the doctor-patient model (abandoning collaborative humanistic values) are constant hazards. Partnering with and getting feedback from professional colleagues and taking time-outs for spiritual cleansing and skill rejuvenation are essential to practitioner survival.

- Operational managers and human resource professionals can become much more effective when adding humanistic consulting practices to their management repertoires. Organization development practitioners do not have a monopoly on humanistic management. If OD practitioners are not eager to share their processes and techniques, they are not really practicing humanistic consultation and should be replaced.

- Some practitioners and many more academics tend to overdose on the concept of a pure *behavioral science*. It is an impressive term, and there is a scientific basis for many interventions, particularly those associated with behaviorism. However, for the working practitioner, relevant consultation is much more of an art than a science. Compassion, intuition, and the ability to form a client-centered helping relationship are the requisite competencies.

6. Organizational Behavior: OD's Academic Cousin

"On the whole, the humanistic model is more philosophical than scientific."—*Fred Luthans*

First, a differentiation between the terms. Organization *development* is focused on the development of organizations. Organizational *behavior* is concerned with human behavior within organizations. Students, managers, academics, and sometimes practitioners often confuse the two. So, for the reader who insists on erroneously using *organizational* development, now you can go for it. The correct term for organization development's academic cousin is, indeed, *organizational* behavior.

To pioneering organizational behavior theoretician Fred Luthans, organizational behavior is a "science," grounded in behaviorism: the stimulus-response paradigm of conditioning. Behaviorism and humanism enjoy and oil and water relationship, a fact that Luthans (1973 216) makes quite clear:

> In essence, the humanistic model is at the opposite extreme from the behavioristic model. Humanism stresses man's intellectual reasoning ability and efforts for self-actualization at the expense of conditioning and immediate stimulation. In other words, while behavioristic man is deterministic, humanistic man has free will…. On the whole, the humanistic model is more philosophical than scientific.

The "Snake Pit" Reality Check

Most organizational behavior academics diffuse the fundamental philosophical chasm between free will and the dehumanizing conditioning posed by Skinner (1972) in his aptly named book, *Beyond Freedom and Dignity*, by focusing their research and teaching on the complex relationships of models, theories, and processes. In the introduction to their textbook on organizational behavior, Nelson and Quick (2006 4), offer this explanation of the chasm, "Human behavior in organizations is complex and often difficult to understand. Organizations have been described as clockworks in which human behavior is logical and rational, but they often seem like snake pits to those who work in them."

Behaviorism discounts free will and posits that with the right conditioning we can be programmed to do almost anything. The end result would be, that with the proper behavioral conditioning, we could work in logical, rational, clockwork organizations. That's not the world that OD practitioners find. They work to change the snake pits, make them freer and more humane, not by conditioning, but by choice. The validity of the snake pit metaphor in real organizations causes many OB professionals to refrain from putting too many eggs in the behavioristic basket.

Same Acorn, Two Intertwined Trees

Regardless of the tension between the polarities of free will and determinism, organizational behavior and organization development have common roots. The acorn was planted in the same soil—a desire to understand human behavior in organizational systems—but two trunks emerged. One, organizational behavior, developed and espoused a number of theories and models based on "science," and articulated them in academic environments. The other, organization development, was based on humanistic principles and focused on application and change in ongoing organizational systems.

In a classic memo to his colleagues, "Organizational Behavior as a Special Field in the Harvard DBA Program" (Vaill 2007), organizational behavior pioneer Fritz Roethlisberger, explored the tension, ambiguity, and necessary cross-fertilization between practice (OD), and theory (OB). As phrased in the title of his autobiography, *The Elusive Phenomena: An Autobiographical Account of My Work in the Field of Organizational Behavior at the Harvard Business School* (Roethlisberger 1977), the connection was important, but not readily apparent.

In middle age the two trunks grew closer together and, "elusive" though the connection may have seemed, began to inform each other. The branches were still, however, separate. Organizational behavior worked with case studies, individual, group, and organizational models and processes developed within a "scientific," university environment. In many business schools a course in organizational behavior is a requirement for both undergraduate and MBA degrees. Organization development evolved toward practitioner-based, hands-on, action research-oriented, processes of facilitating change within live organizations. Today, although there are some universities teaching organization development, there are many more teaching organizational behavior. The blending of the two "elusive" trunks is depicted in figure 4.

Figure 4
Common roots and blending of OB and OD

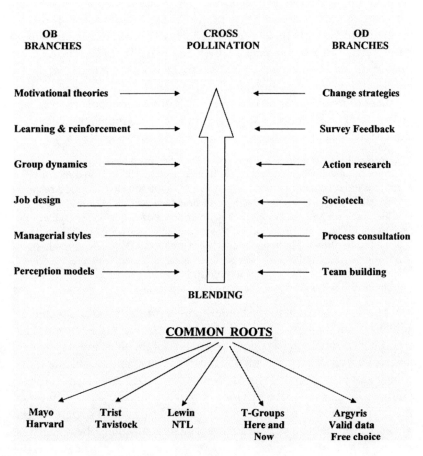

Evolution of Organizational Behavior

CONTRIBUTION OF THE HARVARD BUSINESS SCHOOL

If the child that was to become organization development was fathered by the early NTL pioneers, the mother of organizational behavior was the eclectic soil of the Harvard Business School. Harvard's Fritz Roethlisberger's 1959 memo on organizational behavior as a special field in the Harvard DBA program could be the first recorded use and definition of the term "Organizational Behavior" (Vaill 2007).

There is only a probability that the term organizational behavior was coined at Harvard but there is a certainty that the concept was nurtured there. Just as NTL's early years facilitated the growth of organization development, Harvard's business school provided an environment for the unfolding of organizational behavior. Just as Lee Bradford's (1974) documentation of the early history of NTL illuminated organization development's birth and growing pains, Jeffrey Sonnenfeld's (1985) *The Case of Organizational Study at Harvard: Stages in the Life of an Intellectual Community*, did the same for organizational behavior. If Kurt Lewin was the Abraham whose seed was carried on through diverse tribes of organization development practitioners, the progenitor of organizational behavior was Elton Mayo, who, in the words of Sonnenfeld (1985 34):

> ... worked to create a climate that supported intellectual breath—which applied certain cultural values about social life in organization. He cultivated such disciples as Fritz J. Roethlisberger, Lloyd Warner, George Homans, Conrad Arensberg, Elliot Chappel, William F. Whyte, George Lombard, and David Riesman. With these men and others he held a court of sherry as they discussed the new concepts advanced by Pareto, Piaget, Weber, Durkheim, Janet, Freud, Malinowski and Radcliffe-Brown. The boundaries between economics, sociology, psychology, anthropology, and philosophy were routinely ignored. Field research such as the famed Hawthorne studies provide testing grounds for these theories and training grounds for the teams of social scientists Mayo assembled.

Mayo, an Australian psychologist and a former medical student at Edinburgh and London, came to Harvard in 1926. He pushed beyond the prevailing scientific management orientation of the time and was deeply concerned with social problems and the impact of organizations and technologies on people. In this regard, he not only moved away from Luthan's concept of organizational behavior as a purely empirical science, but also aligned himself with NTL's Lee Bradford's focus on broad social change. Under Mayo, the field that was to become organizational behavior was eclectic, socially-oriented, and labeled as "entrepreneurial" (Sonnenfeld 40).

FRAGMENTATION AND DEFINITIONAL AMBIGUITY

Fritz Roethlisberger led the group of scholars and teachers who followed Mayo. They continued the boundary-spanning scholarship and entrepreneurial culture fostered by Mayo, but, as an unintended consequence, ushered in an era of ambiguous and fragmented focus. In conjunction with the 1983 conference of applied behavioral scientists held on the 75th anniversary of the Harvard Business School, Sonnenfeld (p. 49) summed up the fragmentation:

> To many, the succession of popular topics in organizational behavior smacks of shallow trendiness and a disappointing lack of intellectual integrity. The field has drifted from human relations, to open systems, to contingency models of structure and strategy, to quality of work life, job redesign, to institutional revivalism, and now to human resource management.

But for the focus on OB, Sonnenfeld's assessment echoes Wisebord's (1977) dismay over OD's definitional scope and ambiguity.

During the teen and early adult years of organizational behavior (1970–1985) there was increasing concern over the parameters of the field; what was taught and researched, and how it fit into other management courses and curriculum. The OB journal at the time was *Exchange: The Organizational Behavior Teaching Journal* and there was evidence of this identity crisis in nearly every issue. As an example, Filley, Foster and Herbert (1979 13) wrote:

> There lies no clear definition. Some schools include under the larger rubric of OB: organizational theory, organizational strategy and decision making, organizational development, stress and conflict, or career planning. Others eschew the OB label entirely, choosing instead to identify related courses as "Behavioral Science." They argue for a definition of organizational behavior that is 'sufficiently broad to include all management related concerns about behavior.

It's easy to understand why the multi-disciplinary seeds planted by Mayo and his colleagues caused fragmentation and definitional ambiguity in OB's middle years. To enjoy a comprehensive view, one would have needed an appreciation of the development and evolution of the various schools of psychology, anthropology, sociology, philosophy, educational theory, small group dynamics, communications theory, and economic systems.

This time of directional disparity was reflected in differences both as to what constituted organizational behavior, and how it should be taught. Some, e.g., Hampton, Summer and Weber (1973), viewed organizations as tangible, value-shaping entities and the sole domain of managers. They saw organizations as fixed, stable systems and the role of OB to help managers adapt to the system. In the introduction to their textbook (p. xv) they make this perspective clear: "The manager's system is called the organization ... the objective of this book is to help people learn to fit managerial actions to the nature of organizational behavior." Others, e.g., Athos and Gabarro (1978 xi), took the opposite path and aligned their focus and pedagogical thrust closer to that of organization development:

> We found that our students' learning improved significantly as we shifted our emphasis away from the specific, role-related interpersonal tasks of managers and toward the more universal human dilemmas that managers' face in all their human relationships ... the orientation of this book is phenomenological, humanistic, and pragmatic.

Contemporary Perspective

Today's organizational behavior teachers and researchers do not appear as consumed with definitional boundaries as their predecessors. They are not paralyzed by the organizational implications of the either-or dilemma of behavioral conditioning versus free will. Most current organizational behavior textbooks present theory, research, and case studies in three easily understood, hierarchically ascending categories.

Individual models and processes. The first level focuses on the individual and usually includes personality and perceptual variables along with motivational theories. Topics such as ethics, values, performance management, and stress are often discussed.

Groups and work teams. The second division deals with groups. Topics include work teams and group dynamics. Decision making, leadership, conflict, and negotiation processes are usually part of this grouping.

System-wide processes. The final level involves system-wide processes such as structure, job design, organizational culture, and change management. Organization development is most often covered in this section.

Most contemporary organizational behavior textbooks contain a rich supply of case studies to accompany each of these levels. Although, perhaps not the primary intent, these cases lend themselves to analysis using humanistically grounded organization development lenses. The classic, valid data, free choice, internal commitment to change model can be applied to most of them.

Differences Between OB and OD

It is easy for both the layperson and the practitioner to confuse and misuse the two terms. Organizational behavior and organization development are, in some respects, related, but there are differences in context and application. These are depicted in figure 5.

Figure 5
Organizational behavior and organization development differences

Organizational Behavior	Organization Development
Departments and functions found in colleges and universities.	Departments and functions found in business and non-profit organizations.
Textbooks have a chapter or a section on change management and organization development.	Most textbooks don't have a chapter or a section on organizational behavior.
Organizational behavior professionals don't "practice" OB.	Organization development professionals "practice" OD.
National Journal is The Journal of Management Education.	National Journal is the OD Practitioner.
Called organizational behavior because it deals with human behavior inside organizations.	Called organization development because focus is on organization change and development.
Grounded in research and theory. May include humanistic values.	Grounded in humanistic values. May include research and theory.

Organizational Affiliation and Pedagogical Orientation

Organization development functions and departments are found in business and non-profit organizations. Organizational behavior research and teaching departments are found in universities. There are significantly fewer organization development research and teaching functions in universities and I have yet to find an organizational behavior department in a business. Most organization development textbooks don't have sections or chapters on organizational behavior. Organizational behavior textbooks almost always have a chapter or a section on organization development and change.

PRIMARY IDENTITY AND ARENA OF PRACTICE

Organization development specialists may teach, write, be self-employed or part of a large company, but when they actually *do* OD, they refer to themselves as organization development practitioners. As mentioned previously, that title, *OD Practitioner*, is also the name of the field's national journal. Organizational behavior specialists do not "practice" OB. When organizational behavior people do leave the classroom and do humanistic, not traditional management, consulting, they *do* OD, not OB. Their primary national journal is "*The Journal of Management Education.*" OD professionals mostly practice—OB professionals mostly teach and do research.

Advice and Recommendations

- The roots of organizational behavior and its more applied cousin, organization development, were nourished by the same soil of curiosity and study of human behavior in organizational settings. Two parallel trees emerged from this soil. The OB trunk flourished in academia, focusing on teaching and research. The OD trunk thrived inside ongoing organizations, applying humanistic values and OB research to planned change. The two trees compliment and inform each other, but it is important that OB teachers and OD practitioners understand the boundaries.
- One potential collision of values arises from the core humanistic OD belief in free will and individual choice as opposed to the notion of people as helpless victims of the laws of behavioral conditioning. While some OB professionals are so called "radical behaviorists," most recognize the folly of viewing dynamic human

systems as predictably programmed entities, populated by compliant subjects of behavioral conditioning. OD practitioners operating according to the values of their profession, ground their work in humanistic values. Those OD practitioners who are familiar with the stream of research that has resulted in the laws of behavioral conditioning and those OB academics who grasp the incredible complexity of human systems, are able to reconcile any philosophical divergence and move forward with their specialties.

- The evolution of the two fields followed similar patterns. Both began with founders interested in fundamental social change. Both fragmented and lived with definitional ambiguity and confusing boundaries in the two decades following their inception. And, both seem more settled and focused in contemporary application.

7. Organization Transformation: OD's Radical Cousin

"The predominant modes of operating—profit and return on investment—will have to give way to more global purposes ... create that vision from the perspective of a clearly articulated sense of humanistic values."—*John Adams*

The early founders of organization development and organizational behavior—people like Lewin, Mayo, Bradford, Benne, and Lippitt—were driven by a vision of a better world. With recent memories of the depression and World War II, they sought a process, a way of re-educative change that would make people in organizational systems more humane and able to deal with their conflicts in positive ways. They truly wanted to change the world.

In the early 1980s, organization development had drifted into a maze of techniques and processes that, in many cases, were for sale to the highest bidder, not the system with the highest need. The urge for the transformational, humanistic social change that drove the founders was not uniformly owned by practitioners who often plied their trade in organizations with goals that reinforced and augmented the very systems that the founders wanted to change. On the other side of the dual-trunked tree, organizational behavior had lost the action-oriented eclecticism of Mayo and had taken refuge in the universities where it, too often, became fragmented and political.

It was against this background, with the added impetus of nuclear threat, environmental erosion, and the need for a more democratic global allocation of resources, the "new" thrust and series of ideas that was called Organization Transformation (OT) arose. OT pioneer Ackerman Anderson (2016 61) describes this beginning:

In the early 1980s a group of OD practitioners gathered at a regional OD network conference to explore some emerging questions and patterns we were seeing about change in the organizations we served. John Adams, Harrison Owen, Linda Nelson, Frank Burns, Larry DeBivort, myself and others started a conversation that there was a "new" type of change afoot that was very different to what we were used to seeing.

John Adams edited a book of readings, *Transforming Work* (1984) that was to the emerging field of organization transformation what Bennis, Benne and Chin's *Planning Change* (1961) was to organization development. They were both collections of readings from a diverse group of early influencers; practitioners and theorists who laid out the eclectic boundaries and purposes of their fields.

Thirty-five years have passed since Adam's book and today's concept of organization transformation suffers from a somewhat schizophrenic split in purpose. Adam's book of readings gave the initial public voice to one dimension of the movement—humanistic social transformation. The focus was on political and value-based processes for transforming business organizations to move beyond (p. vii) "the predominant modes of operating—focusing primarily on profit and return on investment." He visualized organizations transforming to become instruments in a transnational effort to deal with world problems. To Adams, OT's relationship with OD was one of having a "broader, more encompassing process—much the in the same way that Einstein's theory of relativity encompassed Newtonian physics."

Today the issues seem even more urgent. In a time of global terrorism, Middle Eastern political chaos and the looming disaster of global warming, the need to use OT technology to fundamentally transform organizational systems is even more compelling than it was in the 1980s. Yet, the primary focus of organization transformation seems to be more directed toward utilizing large systems transformational technologies to make business organizations more competitive and profitable, not as instruments to change the world. Ackerman Anderson (2016 64) describes the need for transformational organization change as more of an economic, market-driven process: "The transformational process is triggered by a profound shift in worldview, with leaders realizing that the organization cannot continue to function or produce what the future demands and must undergo a radical shift to meet the requirements of its changing marketplace."

At one level, the two motivations may be a means and ends division. By transforming in order to survive and meet the needs of a changing global marketplace, business organizations could concurrently usher in a better, more equitable world. However, it is clear that that the contributors in Adam's book of readings were seeking a new social order through transformed organizations, not transforming organizations simply to make more money by better meeting customer needs in a changing marketplace.

Humanistic Social Organization Transformation

Some excerpts from Adam's (1984) seminal book of OT readings demonstrate the idealistic, eclectic, nature of the early years of humanistic social organization transformation.

Vaill (p. 18) writes of moving beyond "the old positivist/objectivist world view," and of "process wisdom for understanding and repairing excesses of western thought."

Nicholl (p. 15) writes of "Multiple models of change and causality that emphasize interactions, patterns, phenomenological intention and love—and by implication, conscious design of our new world."

Kiefer and Senge (p. 70) tell of "metanoic organizations" that derive their name "from a Greek word meaning 'a fundamental shift of mind.'" We learn that the term was "used by early Christians to describe the reawakening of intuition and vision" and that metanoic organizations foster "a deep sense of vision or purposefulness."

Harrison (p. 98) advocates the concept of "conscious evolution where we can begin to participate voluntarily in our own evolution." He articulates a basic issue with transferring humanistic social transformational ideas into the business world when he writes: "Few efforts have been made to apply such ideas to organizations in general or to business in particular. Indeed, at first glance the ideas seem bizarre and otherworldly."

In addition to Adam's book of readings, other thinkers and writers contributed to the humanistic transformational movement of the 1980s. In her *The Aquarian Conspiracy* (1980) Marilyn Ferguson influenced many humanistic social thinkers. Some of the contributors to Adam's book of readings conceptualized the process of transformation as activating and harnessing a preexisting, but difficult to grasp, reality. They would agree with Ferguson's description of the nature of personal and organization transformation. She wrote (p. 20): "We are in the midst of a great transformation—like the charting of a new star, naming and mapping the conspiracy only makes visible a light that has been present all along but unseen because we didn't know where to look."

Ken Wilber (1983 124) presents a perspective of "new sciences" emerging within a paradigmatic shift when he writes of "three eyes," one of the flesh, another of the mind, and a third of contemplation. In his introduction to the "holographic paradigm" he sums up: "We have seen that there might indeed exist the possibility of a 'new and higher' or comprehension-transcendental paradigm, one that at least attempts to include monological sciences, dialogical sciences, mandalic sciences, and contemplative sciences."

Much of the early organizational transformational thinking had to do with the notion of moving from one plane of existence to another: a shift to a new paradigm. Vaill's essay, Process Wisdom for a New Age (1984) describes this shift. I have extrapolated this sense of movement using Vaill's ideas and words in figure 6.

Figure 6
"Process wisdom for a new age" viewed as a paradigmatic movement

FROM	TO
A science based on positivistic data observed →	A process of the observer and the interacting in a phenomenological environment
Science ⟶	Art
Man/person as a "dead fish" ⟶	Man/person as a creator of unique phenomenon
A search for common laws ⟶	An interactive confrontation of the client in his uniqueness
Reductionism—"this is a case of . . ." ⟶	Awe—this individual phenomenon is more than I can ever wholly know
Walling of the underlying truth, beauty, and spirituality of reality in the armor of hard data ⟶	Accepting spirituality as something demanding a response
The manager/consultant as a disinterested measurer ⟶	The manager/consultant as a co-adventurer in "being in the world with responsibility"

DIMENSIONS OF THE QUEST FOR HUMANISTIC, SOCIAL TRANSFORMATION

It was not a recent phenomenon. The hope for new potentialities and possibilities for human organizations has been a part of civilization since recorded language. In the mid–1980s, the words "organization transformation" were new. The type of organization that advocates sought to transform—multinational organizations—seemed new, but history was filled with chronicles of global organizations such as the Catholic Church and the Roman Empire. The roots of social organizational transformation reach back to occurrences such as the French Revolution and Plato's idea of a society ruled by philosopher-kings.

It was grounded in socially oriented paradigmatic change. The Arab Spring of humanistic organization transformation occurred in the mid–1980s. Transformed organizations were seen by practitioners as much more humane, productive, and socially active than in the past. One lens into the "legitimization" of these values were the workshop subjects offered at the fall 1985 national organization development meeting. There was an acceptance of subjects that previously would have been considered too "far out" to have been relevant to many business organizations. There was a session that dealt with "Demons, Deities, Demographics, and Development ... Images of OD as Savior and as Serpent." There was another titled, "Jesus, Meet Kurt Lewin: A Theological Perspective of OD."

It used the language of myth, ritual, and Jungian concepts to create an "in" group. The utilization of Jungian derivatives such as "organizational unconscious," and the use of allegorical, symbolic, and abstract language were common. This had the effect of creating a community of the initiated—those who understood the jargon and were comfortable with its ambiguity—and those who either wouldn't take the time to work through it or were offended by its imprecision and strange vocabulary. Will Durant (1953 294) when writing of the philosopher Hagel's writing style makes a somewhat analogous point, "These are masterpieces of obscurity, darkened by abstractions and condescension of style, by a weirdly original terminology."

Most line managers are able to grasp complex ideas but I don't know many who wouldn't be put off by attempting to operationalize phrases such as "Morphogenetic fields of resonance, beyond space and time, which are hypothesized to organize structure of reality into habitual or usual ways of being," (Adams 1984 277).

In the second edition of Adams' book (1998), he asked the initial contributors to reflect on their writings with the perspective of fourteen years. When reflecting on the difficulty of generating client understanding of his paradigm reframing process, Nicoll (1998 182) raised a languaging and conceptual communication issue that plagues other humanistic

64

transformational practitioners: "Too often, when using this model, I've felt like an English archaeologist with a Summerian map, trying to point out travel highlights to a tour group full of Vietnamese."

It was an outside-in process. Those who wrote and advocated the humanistic organizational transformation revolution of the mid 1980s were either OB academics or OD practitioners. They approached transformation as missionary zealots, knowing what needed to change and engaged organizations as outside advocates. Insiders—line managers, those who spent their lives working inside business organizations—were absent from the ranks of those who wanted to initiate and nurture the transformations of the 1980s. Insiders seemed to be subjects to be converted, not partners to share transformational visions.

When discussing organization transformation Allen and Kraft (1984 36) walked a fine line between external manipulation and the humanistic value of free choice. "Organizations are appropriate places to *instigate* change, because their hierarchical structure makes it possible to *institute* change programs quickly; they comprise great numbers of people, and are capable of grouping people in small units in which the *power of peer influence* is a critical force" (emphasis added).

One of the primary reasons early humanistic social organization transformation had difficulty taking root in business organizations was that managers were wary of overly evangelical practitioners who separated transformation from business objectives. "Higher needs" and "core values" are best defined by the client, not the practitioner.

Economic, Market-Driven Organization Transformation

Fundamental systematic problems such as global warming and disparate distribution of wealth and resources that the early organization transformationists sought to address still plague us, but the focus of humanistic social transformation has shifted to helping business organizations, and the dimensions of that help involve profits and competitive advantage. In the introduction to the second edition of *Transforming Work* (1998 2), Adams warns of the possible unintended consequences of this approach:

> Business is clearly the institution best situated around the world to refine our priorities and practices. It presently is also the primary generator of the pervasive

ecological problems that are crying out for attention ... if those of us who are OD or OT professionals demonstrate excellence in our practices, while operating with these presently prevailing mental models, we may actually be contributing to the collapse of a sustainable human presence on the planet.

DIMENSIONS OF TODAY'S ECONOMIC, MARKET-DRIVEN ORGANIZATION TRANSFORMATION

It's initiated by business leaders. Because of fundamental changes in technology, competition, economic fluctuation, and product life cycles, some business organizations are forced to abandon incremental change and make radical changes in their ways of thinking, operating, and relating to the external environment. They are unlikely to make fundamental changes out of concern only for social responsibility and transformational change is more often stimulated by a new, externally recruited executive (Cummings and Worley 2015 531). Transformational practitioners play a facilitative and advisory role, but the transformational effort is led by line managers.

Transformational practitioners add value by helping align vision and strategy. Wise organizational leaders use qualified practitioners to help align their vision with the design of the transformed organization. Ackerman Anderson (2016 70) writes:

> Getting leaders aligned to what they are trying to accomplish, and what their vision is for their new state is an essential step during launch. They must articulate the factors and principles that are guiding their decision to transform, their design requirements for what the future needs to produce or accommodate, and even they boundary conditions for what cannot change.

Large group interventions are a preferred practitioner strategy. They are effective because of their focus on system wide issues and the involvement of large segments of the organization. Cummings and Worley (2015 309) describe the various forms of these interventions:

> The defining feature of large group interventions ... is the bringing together of large numbers of organization members, often more than a hundred, and a broader range of other stakeholders. Here, conference attendees' work together to identify and resolve organization-wide problems, to design new approaches to structuring and managing the firm.

Large group interventions are a rapidly growing segment of OT. They usually take the form of three to five day-long sessions of employees, customers, board members, and other stake holders. They have labels such as "future search conferences,"—"open space planning,"—"decision accelerators"—and "appreciative inquiry" sessions.

The deeper practitioners move into strategy and structure the more their humanistic marginality is threatened. Large group efforts at organization transformation vary in process and design but, if they are to be considered humanistic consultation, they need to value free choice, participation, and true employee involvement. As organizations necessarily adjust their strategy and structure to accommodate transformation, the OT practitioner can be seduced into crossing a line and joining the ranks of traditional management consultants. As they work with leaders to implement new strategic visions, they face the danger of slipping into a pair-of-hands mode. For those OT practitioners who have crossed the line—"gone over to the dark side"—as described by one colleague, the status and financial rewards are considerable, but they are no longer doing humanistically grounded consultation.

Advice and Recommendations

- The line between what constitutes organization transformation and organization development is blurred with practitioners often using the terms interchangeably. Ackerman Anderson and Anderson (2010 39) make a clear point of demarcation: "Simply said, transformation is the radical shift from one state of being to another, so significant that it requires a shift of culture, behavior and mindset to implement successfully and sustain over time." To the working OD practitioner, the boundary is not always so clear. Some feel that with such a definition, "normal OD" is relegated to a secondary role—a less important level of change.

- The confusion of the relationship and importance of OT to OD is analogous to the ongoing debates over differences between leadership and management—transactional and transformational leadership—and strategy and tactics. One school views OT, transformational leadership, and strategy as deeper, more complex, and of more long-term value. The other perspective is that they are simply points on a continuum and only differentiated by context.

- My view of OT—whether it be the social or economic variety—is congruent with Ackerman Anderson and Anderson's perspective.

It requires a fundamental shift of paradigmatic thinking and organizational culture. That does not diminish the value of OD, for I also agree with the contextual continuum concept: OT is simply OD applied to a radical, system wide, cultural and paradigmatic change.

8. Humanistic Coaching

"Coaching is about challenging and supporting
people, giving them the gift of your
presence."—*Robert Hargrove*

Sometimes called "executive coaching," although the person receiving the coaching is often a manager or an individual contributor, coaching is a rapidly growing field (Goldsmith and Lyons 2005) and a natural fit for humanistic consultants. There are two types of coaching. The first involves a one-on-one relationship where an external coach forms a helping relationship with an internal client (Feldman and Lankau 2005). The other involves operational managers within organizations engaging in helping relationships with their fellow employees (Kouzes and Posner 2005). In both cases, effective coaching as Hargrove (1995 11) writes: "is about challenging and supporting people, giving them the gift of your presence." The bestowing of this gift requires the application of the humanistic values of participation, personal accountability, and free choice.

The Big Three Humanistic Coaching Derailment Factors

At a recent professional gathering of experienced consultants, the moderator asked participants to describe "what kind of work they were doing these days." The response was both surprising and distressing. The surprise came with the discovery that almost everyone in the room claimed to be doing some kind of "executive coaching." The distress came with the knowledge that many participants were traditional management consultants and, although effective in their areas of expertise, did not have the training, orientation, or aptitude for maintaining the special kind of helping relationship necessary for effective humanistic coaching.

With the de-layering of organizations and expanded spans of control, the coaching and mentoring role previously performed by managers is increasingly being farmed out. It is a rapidly expanding field of practice but, unfortunately, many organizations are not getting what they are paying for. In some cases external coaches end up doing more harm than good. There are three primary reasons many coaching efforts run into trouble and why well intentioned coaches come off the track. They are victims of one or more of the big three coaching derailment factors. Each can be viewed from the perspective of the coach, the client, and the humanistic underpinnings of the coaching relationship.

Confusion, Collusion, and Lack of Clarity as to Who Is the Client

The following is a condensed version of a meeting between me, a CEO, and his vice president of human resources.

"We've heard a lot of good things about your coaching work, and we've got a senior vice president we'd like you to change," said the HR vice president.

"Technically, he's great, but he doesn't have good people skills," added the CEO.

"What do you want me to do?" I asked.

"You know, fix him, help him change because he's in trouble," responded the HR vice president.

"We don't have a lot of time to waste. How long would it take to get some tangible results?" asked the CEO, first looking at his watch, then to his desktop calendar.

When I didn't respond, the HR vice president jumped in. "We've got a corporate budget to cover these kind of things. The cost of this effort would be invisible to him so your fee shouldn't be a reason for him to say no." He smiled and winked at the CEO.

"How's that for a deal?" said the CEO.

It was the kind of a deal I would pass up. It wasn't congruent with humanistic values, the way I believe coaches should function, or the prognosis for success in any helping relationship. The lessons from that meeting are as follows:

Lessons for the practitioner. Contract with the person receiving the coaching, not his boss, an HR professional, a management committee, or any other third party. Contracting with anyone else will violate the concept of free choice and pollute any chance of authentic results. Who was the client in the above example? It certainly was not the person who would be the focus of the coaching. It was the boss, who, I discovered after further discussion, hadn't really told the person he was in trouble. I also discovered that the vice president of HR had already determined that the person would be eventually terminated and was more interested in documenting the file and creating the impression that the organization had done all it could do to save the employee, than achieving any positive outcome.

Lessons for the client. If you are told you should be working with a coach, find out why the organization thinks you need one. I am often amazed that otherwise smart and analytical executives simply comply with the suggestion that they *need* a coach and passively accept the coach offered up by the company. My advice is to do some digging. Why do they think you need coaching? What needs to change? Is there a message your boss can't or won't deliver? If you do choose to work with a coach be assertive of your client status. If possible choose your own coach, if this isn't possible at least get veto power. It makes it much more professional if you pay the tab for coaching out of your own budget. If there is a corporate cost center, at least get visibility as to what the company is paying. Above all, insist on the three coaching C's:

- *Clarity.* You, not the organization, are the client.
- *Confidentiality.* All information is yours alone and there are no reports by the coach to your boss or others as to progress that you don't know about and endorse.
- *Control.* You are in charge of the process, not the coach or the boss, and you are the only one qualified to decide if it is helpful.

Lessons for humanistic practice. Confusion and, at times, collusion as to the identity of the real client and the purpose of coaching is a primary reason for failed efforts. If the boss or the system is the client, practitioners are not doing coaching, they are helping with performance appraisal, communication facilitation, role definition, or objective setting. All are legitimate consulting efforts, but they definitely are not coaching. Consultants who tell the person who is the target for the coaching that she or he is the client, but really are serving the needs and direction of the boss, are not only unethical, they are setting themselves up for failure and violating humanistic values.

Coaches Enamored of a Single
Model or Approach

A friend, a well published, successful organizational behavior professor, asked for advice. He couldn't understand why he was unable to gain any traction as an executive coach.

"You're a solution looking for a problem," was the reply. Our relationship had long since passed the need to pull punches with each other.

"Your model is great. It got you published and produced a saleable diagnostic instrument, but your model isn't what clients need or want. It doesn't lend itself to a client-centered helping relationship, yet you try to impose it on all clients. Stick to speaking, writing, and selling your instrument. You'll be happier, make more money, and not damage any more coaching clients."

This conversation with my well-published friend provides lessons arising from the second coaching pitfall.

Lessons for the practitioner. Effective executive coaching involves a helping relationship. The requisite ingredients of any humanistic helping relationship are empathy, a non-judgmental approach, and mutual exploration and diagnosis. Dogmatic adherence to a single model or a consultant-centered process will doom an authentic coaching relationship. A review of three past coaching clients will demonstrate the need for an individualized approach. All had different goals and required unique approaches.

One client was involved in a serious exploration of her career options. She wasn't sure she was in the right job or organization. Coaching efforts involved using aptitude measurement instruments, life and career planning activities, and a process of skill and reality assessment.

The second client was working on his presentation and assertiveness skills and coaching involved focused feedback and behavioral rehearsal.

The third had a good chance of becoming CEO of his organization and we worked together to find ways to gain more visibility and credibility with his board.

All three of these efforts were the result of a great deal of listening, mutual exploration, and trust-building. If, like our friend, I had come in and presented a one-dimensional approach using *my* model or *my* approach, I may have felt good about my strategy, but the client's need would not have emerged, and I would have failed.

Lessons for the client. Beware of coaches who want to sell you on a single process or *their* solution to *your* issue. An effective coach will be an outstanding listener, much more interested in your ideas—your definition of what would be helpful—your hopes, dreams and aspirations, than their model or process. Be particularly wary of coaches who use athletic models and metaphors. Athletic coaching is a totally different genre than executive coaching in organizations. Athletic coaches are content experts; they know the game and the skills necessary to optimize performance in the game. Organizational coaches are not content experts; they are process experts. They don't know your product or service, you hire them to help you grow and develop however *you* define growth and development. Athletic coaches are part of the system. Their bottom line is winning. They are paid by the system and fired if they don't rack up the requisite number of wins. Humanistic coaches are outside the system. They are hired by *you* to help *you* decide what winning means to *you*, not the system. There are too many so called executive coaches using the athletic model. It is a shallow cliché. If your coach uses an athletic model drop him and get someone who is a competent humanistic practitioner, not a cartoon character.

Lessons for humanistic practice. As OD pioneer Pat Williams, in one of his memorable maxims to his OD graduate students said, "Help is defined by the person receiving the help, not the person giving it." Humanistic coaching is a helping relationship, and like all helping relationships, requires mutuality, openness, and focus on the client as a unique individual. Gimmicks, dogmatic adherence to a technique, and interventions that support the consultant's going-in hypothesis, sabotages authentic coaching.

CREATION OF A DEPENDENCY RELATIONSHIP

The goal of all responsible executive coaches should be to empower their client and withdraw from the relationship. This a major difference from the athletic model where there will always be a coach.

Lessons for the practitioner. Coaches should be aware of, and reject the temptation to create a dependency relationship with their client. This perverts the coaching role, diminishes both the coach and the client, and trivializes the coaching process. A coach should never stay in a helping relationship for the money. The goal should not be, as articulated by one misguided but honest consultant "a long-term relationship with the client and a steady stream of income for me."

Lessons for the client. Insist on a client/coach prenuptial. Make sure you and your coach are on the same wave-length as to when and how the coaching relationship will end. It's easy to become comfortable and dependent. Resist the temptation to prolong the relationship. It's important and ennobling for you to solo. Coaching is much more effective when it is bounded in time and by pre-determined objectives. Set these goals and limits early in the coaching process and stick to them. It is not good for you or your coach to create a long-term dependency relationship. A competent humanistic practitioner will help facilitate a healthy separation. If your coach overstays her welcome and won't let go, fire her.

Lessons for humanistic practice. Coaching is a temporary and artificial process and it is essential that a termination plan be part of the initial contracting. Colleagues who tell of remaining with the same client for multiple-year coaching engagements raise red flags in terms of their adherence to the humanistic value of client empowerment. It is acceptable to withdraw and return to monitor progress and help the client formulate new goals, but the strategy should always be to empower the client and terminate the relationship. Coaches and visiting relatives have something in common with dead fish: they begin to smell if they stay too long.

The Triangle Coaching Model

Although humanistic coaching practitioners are grounded in the classic Argyris (1973) formula of valid data, free choice, and internal commitment, many tend toward a favorite component at the expense of the other two. Some overdose on data, others help clients pursue an overwhelming maze of choices and options, while still others prematurely press for closure and goal setting. The triangle coaching model (Noer, 2006) in figure 7 was developed as a practical guideline to help coaches maintain balance in the three dimensions of coaching.

CENTER FOR CREATIVE LEADERSHIP ROOTS

The Center for Creative Leadership has been offering leadership development experiences for over forty years using a three pronged approach (McCauley, Moxley, and Van Velsor 1998). The first involves assessment: measurement, feedback, and benchmarking. The second is challenge: action planning and goal setting. The final prong is support: non-judgmental facilitation and empathy. These three dimensions are a derivative of

Figure 7
Triangle coaching model

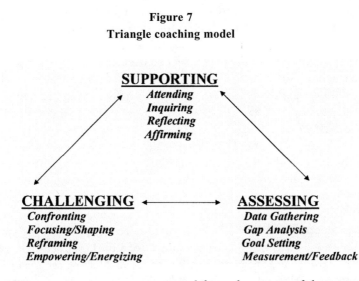

Argyris' interventionist components and form the points of the triangle coaching model.

THE THREE INTERACTIVE COACHING DIMENSIONS

Supporting. The supporting dimension involves creating an interpersonal context that facilitates trust, openness, respect and understanding. The four enabling behaviors are attending (using body language, voice tone, and physical setting to reduce defensiveness), inquiring (asking questions to elicit information and clarify perspective), reflecting (promoting clarity and demonstrating understanding by the coach stating in her own words what she thinks the person being coached is saying or feeling), and, affirming (directly communicating that the coach believes the person being coached has the ability to change, learn, or develop). These behaviors are found in Kinlaw's (1996) Superior Coaching Model.

Challenging. This dimension involves helping the person being coached confront obstacles, re-conceptualize issues, and move forward with renewed energy and self-reliance. The behavioral components are confronting (helping the person being coached face and understand issues, behaviors, or perceptions that are blocking her), focusing/shaping (moving the coaching conversation from the general to the specific toward actionable outcomes), reframing (helping the person being coached examine and validate her assumptions and inferences) and, empowering/energizing (helping the person being coached develop an increased sense of purpose and self-reliance). Hargrove (1995 53–82) presents some excellent examples of confronting in his discussion of transforming "rut" stories to "river" stories. Kinlaw (1996, 33–36) provides an overview of shaping a coaching conversation. Ross' (1994, 242) discussion of a ladder of inference is helpful in understanding reframing inferences and assumptions. Whitworth, Kimsey-House and Sandahl (1998 115) present a useful perspective of empowering/energizing.

Assessing. This set of coaching behaviors involves methods used by the coach to involve the person being coached in collecting information and setting goals. From a humanistic coaching perspective, it is important that this be a collaborative effort, not just done by the coach. The behaviors are data gathering (securing information that will be of use to the person being coached), gap analysis (utilizing differences between the current reality and the client's objectives to stimulate action), goal setting (making concrete plans) and, measurement/feedback (establishing criteria to assess progress and developing mechanisms for feedback on behavioral change).

THE PRICE OF UNBALANCED COACHING

There is no prescribed sequence to the triangle model. Some inexperienced coaches have tried to impose a sequential approach where, for example, a coach would always begin with supporting behaviors, then move to assessing, and conclude a coaching session with challenging. Authentic coaching doesn't occur that way. The model is interactive, situational, and dynamic. A coach can start anywhere and end anywhere. What's important is that there is balance and all behaviors are demonstrated.

Overuse of one dimension at the expense of the other two results in a distorted process. Over-reliance on supporting behavior can result in an open, trusting coaching session with little commitment to action or measurement. Too much focus on challenging can cause confusion, defensiveness, and unfocused action. Over-use of assessing behaviors can lead to data overload and "analysis paralysis." A balanced relationship of the three dimensions is depicted in figure 8.

The Power of Truth Tellers

Wise organizational leaders cultivate internal "truth tellers." A truth teller is someone inside an organization who, to use baseball umpire lan-

Figure 8
Balanced coaching

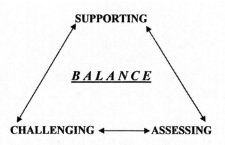

SUPPORTING

BALANCE

CHALLENGING ←————→ ASSESSING

guage, "calls them the way he sees them." On the leader's part, it requires trust that the truth teller isn't using his role to gain personal power or influence. For the truth teller, it requires the courage to give direct and unfiltered feedback to the leader. The most effective internal truth tellers have three characteristics: they are tuned into what is going on at all levels of the organization—top, middle, and bottom—they are secure with no personal ax to grind, and they have faith that the leader trusts them enough to hear and weigh *their* truth which may not be the same as the leader's truth. Truth telling can be as simple as giving feedback to the leader on the unintended, dysfunctional reaction to her comments in a meeting, or as complex as helping her understand the effects of an ingrained management culture on the retention of millennial employees.

While external humanistic coaches often interact with clients at deeper, more personal levels than internal truth tellers, they must find ways to partner with them and honor their relationship with the leader. This avoids any conflicts over who has the leader's ear, and enlists the truth teller to reinforce the coach's interventions after she departs. I have found it helpful to consider the truth teller and the leader as co-clients. This adds another voice to mutual diagnosis and allows the truth teller to play a direct role in the leader's change goals. I, for example, helped a truth teller "contract" with a leader to observe his staff meetings and give feedback after each meeting on the leader's progress in allowing more participation and giving more "airtime" to his direct reports.

In those cases where there is no truth teller, it is extremely useful to help the leader identify one. Humanistic practitioners can add value by helping in the selection, training, and role expectations of new internal truth tellers. Truth tellers can be found in all organizational functions.

Most, from my experience, come out of operational management or human resources. The nurturing and, if needed, selection of internal truth tellers is an important part of the external coach's exit strategy.

Advice and Recommendations

- If you are a consultant and tempted to join the rapidly growing ranks of executive and management coaches, it's important that you bring your humanistic values with you. Coaching is a helping relationship and in humanistic practice it's essential to adhere to Pat William's dictum to Pepperdine MSOD classes: "Help is defined by the helpee, not the helper."

- If you are an operational manager and considering the retention of a coach, do your due diligence before retaining the first one you see. Look for marginality—is she sufficiently different than you to add value? Look for an exit plan—how long will she stay and when will you both know it's time for her to leave? Look for flexibility— is she willing to diagnostically partner with you without a preconceived solution to a problem she may not understand?

- The triangle coaching model is a useful frame of reference for client/consultation communication. Going over the model together prior to the decision to engage clarifies expectations and provides a tangible roadmap for the relationship.

9. Leadership Development

> "Leadership is authenticity, not style."
> —*Bill George*

Leadership development is a big business with a questionable return on investment. Annual expenditures vary but, by any count, the numbers are staggering—well over $170 billion by one estimate—and the reported results are disappointing (Myatt 2012). The field represents an expanding opportunity for humanistic consultants to ply their trade but they first must avoid some hazards and stake out some boundaries.

Humanistic Practice Fits Leadership, Not Management, Development

Part of the reason that organizations are often disappointed with the results of leadership development activities is that much of what is labeled *leadership* development is really *management* development and the skills that are developed are based on a competency list over 100 years old. Humanistic practitioners can play an important role in leadership development but should leave management development to traditional consultants.

Although management and leadership activities overlap, there is a significant contextual difference between the two. The classic differentiation by Peter Drucker and Warren Bennis that management is "doing things right and leadership is doing the right things" (Covey 1989, 101) has a nice ring to it but is difficult to pin down. A clearer differentiation is analogous to the contrast between what Burns (1978) and Bass (1994) call *transformational* leadership and *transactional* leadership. Transformational leaders provide inspiration and possess the skills to articulate and stimulate acceptance and commitment to a galvanizing future vision. They are compelled to change the status quo by highlighting problems within the current system

79

and formulating a compelling vision of what a new organization could be. In contrast, transactional leaders focus on promoting stability rather than promoting change. They lead by clarifying and monitoring existing processes and cultural norms.

The classic definition of management doesn't fit either today's transactional or transformational leadership requirements. It lists controlling, evaluating, directing, and planning and was initially postulated by Henri Fayol in 1916 (Fayol 1949). The management and leadership environment is much different than Fayol's time in the early 1900s, yet many organizations and business schools remain wedded to his old definition. To be relevant to the organizational and interpersonal issues in today's environment, managers must move beyond Fayol's list and develop leadership competences in helping, empowering, coaching, and visioning. This shift is shown in in figure 9. Facilitating the development of these skills is an appropriate role for humanistic consultants.

Figure 9
Movement from dated to relevant management competencies

FROM		TO
Controlling	⟶	Helping
Evaluating	⟶	Empowering
Directing	⟶	Coaching
Planning	⟶	Visioning

Management development inside organizations emphasizes the same skills taught in most MBA and undergraduate business education curricula. Financial planning, accounting, strategy, supply chain management, marketing, and economics are primary subjects. Not to depreciate the value of competencies in these areas, but humanistic consultants engaged in programs focused on these subjects are working against their professional grain and involved in traditional management training, not humanistic leadership development. They can add significantly more value by concentrating on helping develop relevant leadership skills.

As is shown in figure 10, as employees ascend the organizational hierarchy, the value of technical and managerial skills diminishes and the importance of leadership skills increases. In order to provide the necessary vision, inspiration, and trust in today's dynamic global environment, leaders need

Figure 10
Relationship of skill to level

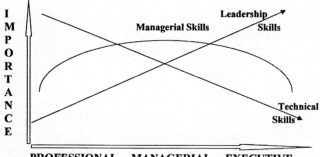

self-awareness, interpersonal competence, and behavioral value congruence. Helping develop and hone these skills is the territory of humanistic practitioners.

The Danger of Over-Valuing Leadership Definition and Under-Valuing Context

As Rost (1991) points out, there are hundreds of conflicting definitions of leadership in both the academic and practitioner worlds. Rost views this as lamentable—a problem needing resolution—I see it as an understandable artifact of the complexity and context-dependent reality of the leadership process. At the expense of their clients, some practitioners—often those of the traditional management consulting variety—spend too much time attempting to articulate universal leadership traits and competency lists, and too little working to understand the organizational context of leadership. The military squad leader in a combat situation has a very different context of leadership behavior than the chief financial officer of an international corporation. The CEO of a non-profit staffed by volunteers faces very different leadership and motivational issues than the head of a growing high tech firm staffed by highly mobile, in-demand professionals.

Adhering or attempting to emulate one style or definition of leadership is not congruent with humanistic practice. Humanistic practitioners must help clients focus on their individual, unique style and develop authentic behaviors. As George (2003 11) writes: "Leadership is authenticity, not style ... not what the experts in Corporate America teach. They describe the styles of leaders and suggest you adopt them. This is the opposite of authenticity."

Five Ways Humanistic Practitioners Can Add Developmental Value

The relevant humanistic practitioner can add the most value by helping her clients develop leadership competencies that fit the unique context of their organizations. More importantly, from the perspective of humanism, they can help clients discover a path to self-understanding and leadership behaviors congruent with their own values rather than adhering to an externally prescribed list of traits or behaviors.

NURTURE SELF ASSESSMENT AND LIFE PLANNING

The Center for Creative Leadership is perennially recognized by publications such as *Business Week* and the *Financial Times* as an award-winning leadership research and educational institution. As indicated in Chapter 8, they use a derivative of Argyris' valid data, free choice, and internal commitment model as a foundation for their leadership development activities. They call it assess, challenge, and support. Central to their humanistic grounding is facilitating self assessment and self-directed change. Hernez-Broome and Hughes (2004 27) write:

> Much leadership development feedback naturally affects how people think about *themselves* not just their interactions with others. Similarly, it can lead to re-evaluations of many aspects of one's life, not just one's role as a leader. It can affect the whole person. The Center for Creative Leadership began during the heyday of the human potential movement, and its ideals and educational philosophy still reflect a commitment to the value of *self-directed change and growth* (albeit informed by knowledge about the needs of the organization).

FACILITATE CLASSROOM INSIGHTS

Although meaningful leadership development involves much more than classroom training sessions (McCauley, Moxley and Van Velsor

2003), a number of humanistic consultants spend significant time in classroom environments as part of corporate, university executive, and private (such as The Center for Creative Leadership) education programs. In congruence with the core values of humanism, practitioners do much more facilitation than "teaching" and help participants arrive at personal insights as opposed to checking off their understanding of prescribed curriculum. This facilitative, client-centered approach is sometimes initially uncomfortable to participants who are conditioned to traditional "I teach,-you learn" educational experiences, but most soon appreciate the value and enjoy the freedom. One helpful design option has been to pair a humanistic practitioner with a more traditional classroom instructor.

Help Leaders Make Sense Out of Assessment Instruments and Processes

Many leadership development programs utilize a variety of personality tests and 360-degree (boss-peer-subordinate-self) feedback instruments. Some utilize roleplays and small group exercises (such as situations that require collaboration and those that stimulate competitiveness). When leaders conditioned to having their own way and not subject to feedback that's different than their self-image receive disconfirming feedback, there is natural defensiveness and rationalization. Humanistic practitioners can be of enormous assistance by helping feedback recipients understand the purpose of roleplays and instruments, put the results in perspective, and give the participant time, psychological space, and options as to what to do about the feedback. Once the participant leaders decide on a course of action, the practitioner can be of further help in assisting with goal setting and follow-up planning.

Help Process Learnings from Job Assignments

With the publication of *The Lessons of Experience* (1988), McCall, Lombardo and Morrison documented what many savvy executives knew all along: the most effective leadership development occurs on the job—through rotational assignments such as moving from a line to a staff role, changing from leading traditional operations to leading start-ups, and learning from both good and bad bosses. The benefits of planned, developmental job assignments can result in competitive advantages as well as better prepared leaders (Ohlott 2004).

Humanistic practitioners can play a valuable coaching role by helping leaders derive the most developmental value from rotational assignments. By consciously articulating what they learned and reflecting on the implications of that learning, clients can maximize the takeaways from their experience. Through reflective questions such as, "What did you learn from that difficult boss?" "What would you do differently?" "How did that staff assignment help you understand how to work with responsibility but no real authority?" clients can channel their new insights into future leadership roles. Some practitioners also ask their leader/clients to use journaling to document their new insights.

Most developmental assignments require those being developed to operate outside their comfort zone. Practitioner consultants can serve as a sounding boards, help clients adjust, provide perspective and empathetic coaching.

HELP PREVENT CAREER DERAILMENT

As leaders ascend into higher organizational levels, they face the risk of behaviors that could cause career derailment (Noer, 2016). The classic research by McCall and Lombardo (1983) is as true today as it was over 30 years ago. The higher one rises, the more seemingly small problems of the past become more pronounced and threaten derailment. Difficulty building and maintaining a team, a tendency toward a bullying, intimidating style, and only hiring in one's own image are pervasive derailment hazards.

Some humanistic practitioners have formed successful coaching relationships with leaders they have encountered through developmental programs. By helping them hold up mirrors to see their career-limiting behaviors, they have assisted in preventing derailment and encouraged more organizationally beneficial and personally empowering behavioral patterns.

Threats to Authentic Leadership Development

Authenticity is a fundamental value to the humanistic consultant and there is a common frustration among many that their efforts to help develop leaders involve just going through the motions and don't really "take" inside clients' organizations. There are some systemic organizational cultural issues that lend a degree of validity to these frustrations.

EROSION OF SUCCESSION PLANNING SYSTEMS

There was a time—twenty to thirty years ago—when most large organizations had elaborate succession planning systems, complete with back-up organizational charts and individual development plans. The mantra of many middle managers was something like, "I need to develop a successor so I can move up." Things have changed. Today, many organizations have abandoned formal succession planning systems and have no framework for individual development plans. The middle management pool as a percentage of organizational population has drastically shrunk. Rather than worrying about developing back-ups, middle managers are worried about holding onto their jobs. There two primary reasons for this shift.

Flattened organizational structures. Reengineering as outlined by Hammer and Champy (1993) has struck. Organizations are flatter with much wider spans of control and many fewer managers. The past role of middle management was to communicate between the workers and the executives. With flatter organizations and computers to facilitate communication, the middle management function has atrophied, and with it the necessity for concern over back-ups.

Short term planning and temporary systems. Although often producing elaborate, long-range strategic plans, in reality many organizations are operating on a quarter-to-quarter timeframe driven by short term profits. In an environment of mergers, acquisitions, reorganizations, downsizings, and rapid advances in technology, organizations are temporary systems that don't have the requisite stability and predictability for valid succession planning.

PERCEPTION OF EMPLOYEES AS COSTS TO BE REDUCED, NOT ASSETS TO BE DEVELOPED

Despite corporate pronouncements of the need to find ways to better engage employees, there exists an underlying perception—politically incorrect to publicly articulate—among a surprising number of managers that people are short-term costs to be minimized, not long-term assets to be developed and nurtured over a career. This is a legacy of reengineering and the layoff culture that began in the 1980s. Complicating matters is the reality that in the U.S. and a few Western European countries, organizations don't want life-time employees and a growing number of employees don't plan to be "lifers."

Those involved in leadership development activities find themselves operating in a form of cultural-lag where organizations are advocating the development of leaders but often don't have the stability or infrastructure to fully utilize them. For the optimistic practitioner this means they are helping develop leaders for organizations other than the ones paying the cost and the mismatch doesn't bother them. For others, the incongruity can lead to frustration and a quest to seek another outlet in which to ply their trade.

Advice and Recommendations

- There is a difference between management development and leadership development and humanistic practitioners are far better suited to helping nurture and develop leaders. If you are a humanistic practitioner and you find yourself working on developing managerial skills of controlling, evaluating, directing and planning as opposed to competencies in helping, empowering, coaching, and visioning, you are working against the grain of your calling and in congruence with traits that Frenchman, Fayol, listed 100 years ago.

- If you are an operational manager seeking help in developing leaders who will be relevant to the future, make certain you focus on programs, consultants, and educational experiences that move beyond transactional managerial skills. Figure 10 makes two persuasive points. The importance of managerial competencies peaks at the hierarchal midpoint and declines rapidly further up the ladder. Conversely, the importance of leadership skills grows exponentially by level. If your organization fits the prevailing pattern, middle management is in decline and you need to spend your money on developing leaders, not more managers.

- Context is important. There is no universal definition of leadership and each organizational purpose and mission is unique. One size does not fit all and leadership development activities need to fit the context and culture (desired more than current) of your organization.

- Self-understanding and internally guided development is an essential component of humanistic leadership development. Practitioners can make a lasting contribution by helping clients discover a path to self-understanding and leadership behaviors congruent with their own values rather than adhering to an externally pre-scribed list of traits or behaviors.

- Flattened organizational structures, short-term planning, tempo-rary systems, and the changing psychological employment contract have led to the erosion of succession planning systems. Realistic humanistic practitioners frame their help in a philosophy of devel-oping leaders with competencies that, despite contextual differ-ences, will span the boundaries of any individual organization.

PART TWO

INFLUENCE OF THERAPEUTIC AND PHILOSOPHIC MODELS

"Practically all therapeutic, quasi-therapeutic,
educational and quasi-educational activities
may include elements of learning, feeling better,
and behaving differently."—*Stephen Appelbaum*

The first three chapters in this section explore the blurred boundaries between therapeutic and consultation techniques. Most humanistic practitioners do not contract for, don't perform, and are not licensed to do full-blown psychotherapy. Many, however, employ processes that are derivatives of therapeutic approaches, often without knowing their origin.

Humanistic consultants owe it to themselves and their clients to have a basic understanding of the theoretical base that supports their interventions. Using a model of therapeutic approaches, the intervention strategies of the major schools of therapy are explored along with their implications to the practitioner.

Humanistic practice has roots in that branch of philosophy—existentialism—that deals with our purpose and necessity to create meaning for our lives. The fourth chapter in this part explores the impact of existential theory on the three dimensions of Argyris' intervention model, the existential imperative for marginality, and Kierkegaard's notion of a leap of faith as a way to understand practitioner adherence to humanistic values.

10. Reflections on Therapy and Consultation

"There is nothing that a psychotherapist does that
a counselor does not do."—*Raymond Corsini*

I am are now aware that early in my exposure to individual coaching and leadership development, many of my mentors—both practitioners and educators—borrowed rather heavily from the traditional psychotherapies, particularly Gestalt techniques and Rogerian approaches. I was taught the "empty chair technique," and how to help clients complete "unfinished business." I learned that empathy and unconditional positive regard were preconditions to a helping relationship. It was years later, after exposure to some of the basics of Gestalt and Rogerian theory, that I recognized the sources of these techniques. I have also come the conclusion that that many of these educators and mentor-practitioners didn't have a conceptual grounding in the theories and approaches of the common psychotherapies and little knowledge of from whence originated their techniques and processes. It was as though the roots of these practitioner practices were lost in the mists of history. This section is intended to clear some of these mists.

Counseling, Coaching and Therapy: Fuzzy Boundaries

The boundaries of the techniques used in therapy, coaching, leadership development, and some forms of group intervention are ambiguous and overlapping. Most practitioners learned their craft, as did I, through a combination of formal training and informal apprenticeship. Too many lack a basic knowledge of the differing schools of therapy or an appreciation that they, in their OD and OT work, are, often "doing" derivatives of therapy. This, and the following two chapters, provide a brief overview of the common approaches to therapy and their relationship and implications to the humanistic practitioner.

At a professional convention, I asked a cross-section of coaching and management development practitioners if they did any form of therapy. Almost all denied—some vigorously—engaging in any type of therapeutic relationship with their clients. One reason was an understandable concern with licensing requirements and possible legal issues. Some participants expressed a concern over a perceived lack of academic qualifications and fear of being seen as imposters. All readily agreed that they engaged in various forms of "counseling" with their clients. There was, however, no common agreement concerning the boundaries between therapy and counseling.

A differentiation offered by some was that the primary difference between therapy and coaching had to do with internal versus external change objectives—internal change was deemed the task of therapy, while external observable behavior was the province of humanistic coaches. Years before that conference a similar differentiation was made by a graduate school instructor in a course called "Advanced Techniques in Counseling." She indicated the difference was in "contract setting," with counseling focusing on external goals and therapy having internal insight and awareness goals. That explanation didn't make sense to me then and makes even less today with the perspective of many years of practice. Therapist Corsini (2000 2) offers a different viewpoint which is more in line with my own experience. He writes: "They are the same qualitatively; they differ only quantitatively. There is nothing that a psychotherapist does that a counselor does not do."

Blindly Borrowed Techniques

Humanistic practitioners of both OD and OT persuasions don't, and shouldn't, contract for full-blown therapeutic interventions. Unless licensed and trained, they can do a client more harm than good. If licensed and wanting to practice therapy, they should hang out a shingle and not pose as an OD/OT practitioner. It is, however, obvious that humanistic practitioners do use some techniques that are grounded in therapy and equally obvious that many don't know the roots of their techniques. I have observed practitioners using roleplaying and group work (à la Adler); "I" statements and guided fantasy (à la Gestalt); non-evaluative listening and positive support (à la Rogers); and using the Meyers-Briggs Type Indicator without understanding the Jungian theory upon which it is based.

They may not be aware of the foundational theory but when practitioners are doing their best one-on-one coaching and counseling work they are, in fact, engaged in a quasi-therapeutic, helping relationship with the "other." They are drawing upon some internal therapeutic model to facilitate situational congruence and allow them to function at this level. Raising these mental models to a conscious level by connecting them to common therapeutic approaches can only help practitioners be more effective coaches.

The Special Needs of Top Managers

Without explicitly knowing its Rogerian roots, practitioners sometimes achieve a therapeutic relationship with top managers simply by non-evaluative listening. Senior executives are quite often emotionally isolated and unable to vent their true feelings with others for fear of looking vulnerable or feeling manipulated. As one CEO said during a coaching session, "If my board knew how I really felt—how insecure I am—how unsure I am about our strategy—they'd fire me. I can't share my feelings with my staff. Some would be terrified and a couple would try to use them against me."

The role of a senior executive is lonely and extremely stressful. A surprising number bottle up their feelings, don't seek outside help, and don't externalize their emotions with spouses or friends. A humanistic practitioner sometimes becomes their only outlet. Those who are able to form an empathetic helping relationship provide an incredibly powerful form of therapeutic relief. For some well-known guru-like practitioners, this is their only intervention. Are they doing therapy? Are they doing counseling? The answers are yes, and yes. Corsini (2000 1) comments on the confusing definition of what actually constitutes therapy:

> Psychotherapy cannot be defined with any precision. If we examine various theories and procedures we find a truly bewildering set of ideas and behaviors. The concept that psychotherapy goes into depth while counseling does not is gainsaid by such procedures as behavior modification which explicitly does not go into depth. Behavior modifiers could hardly be called counselors since they do not council. And when we have a term such as nondirective counseling, we have a sematic absurdity if one thinks about it long enough.

Shared Ambiguity: Lack of a Universal Model

The world of therapy, much like the worlds of OD and OT, is filled with a myriad of conflicting and overlapping interventions and modules of practice. Corsini (p. 1) comments on the contradictions: "It is important to note that what one authority considers to be psychotherapy may be completely different from how another person sees the process.... A and B may be doing completely different and contradictory things, both are doing psychotherapy." In his chronicle of non-psychoanalytic therapies, *A Psychoanalyst Explores the Alternate Therapies* (Appelbaum 1993 472) concludes that when comparing the effectiveness of traditional psychotherapy with alternative processes it is best to follow Scott Fitzgerald's advice and hold two opposite ideas in your mind at the same time and still retain the capacity to function.

Two organizations undergoing "development" by different practitioners could experience very different processes, depending on the point of entry, the diagnosis of the root cause problem, and the orientation and experience of the practitioner. The person undergoing therapy with a traditional psychoanalytically-oriented therapist, and another going through behavior therapy are likewise involved in two diverse conceptual paradigms.

In an articulation of the complexity of assessing therapeutic outcomes, Strupp and Hadley (1977 196) point out that there are differences in what constitutes mental health and therapeutic evaluation criteria from the perspectives of society as a whole, the client, and the mental health professional. Society looks for conformity with social norms, the individual looks for symptom relief, and the mental health professional seeks "fit" within her theory. Since all three of these factors must be in alignment for all parties to agree, there is a probability that "the same individual may simultaneously be judged as mentally healthy or mentally ill and, correspondingly, his therapeutic experiences may be judged as positive or negative depending on who is evaluating the patient." The same probability of differing prognoses exists when different practitioners assess an organization's health. When possible, the wise consultant will turn to colleagues for diagnostic assistance before moving into an intervention.

An Orientation to Therapeutic Approaches

Although OD and OT practitioners don't practice traditional therapy, their interventions—particularly when in coaching relationships—are often based on therapeutic theory. To be a complete practitioner, humanistic consultants owe it to their clients to have a basic understanding of the theoretical base that supports their interventions. Figure 11, the therapeutic orientation model, depicts therapeutic approaches along two dimensions: free will versus determinism and insight versus action. The approaches that are covered in the next two chapters are located in all four quadrants: free will and insightful—Rogers: Person-centered; free will and action oriented—Perls: Gestalt; deterministic and insightful—dynamic: Freud, Adler and Jung; and deterministic and action oriented—Ellis: rational-emotive and Wolpe and Skinner: behavioristic.

Figure 11
Therapeutic orientation model

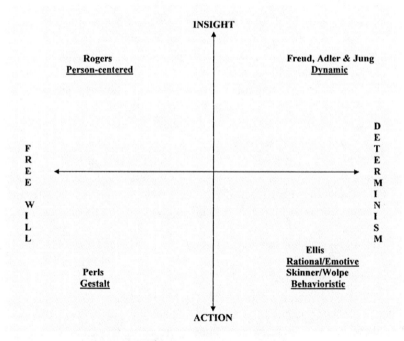

Advice and Recommendations

- If you are a humanistic practitioner and work with clients in an individual coaching relationship, chances are you employ techniques grounded in some dimension of therapy. Chances are also good that you aren't exactly clear how that technique evolved and where it fits in the theoretical framework of therapeutic interventions. In order to be more relevant to your clients and increase your conceptual grounding, you need to invest the time and energy to learn more about the common therapeutic approaches.

- The line between counseling and therapy is an ambiguous continuum. It's not legal or ethical to claim to be doing client therapy, but it's not realistic to deny that you use some therapeutic techniques in your interventions.

- Similar to therapeutic options and outcome evaluations, there is considerable variance in OD and OT intervention strategies and intervention assessments. It is always wise for the lone-wolf practitioner to seek peer feedback on diagnosis and intervention levels and strategies.

- If you are a manager considering employing a coach, it is important that you discover what techniques she will use, their origin, and where she learned them. Don't be reluctant to ask. Some techniques that have therapeutic roots are acceptable. Others, such as long-term, psychodynamic relationships, are definitely out of bounds. If your prospective coach suggests this direction, do not hire her. And, if you need help, find a licensed therapist.

- If you are a senior executive, there is a possibility that you are interpersonally isolated and find it difficult to authentically disclose your feelings and emotions within your firm for fear of manipulation or mistrust. If you don't want to invest in an external therapeutic relationship and find it difficult to talk to your friends or significant other, find a coach who is a skilled, non-judgmental listener. He is not practicing therapy but, if he's good at hearing and, non-judgmentally reflecting back your thoughts and feelings he's absolutely value added.

- If you are a researcher or an OB teacher or student, focus some of your scholarly activity on the relationship, synergy, potential conflicts, and possible new paradigms concerning OD and OT practice and the theoretical orientation of the various therapies.

11. The Big Three: Freud and His Dissident Disciples

"My Echo, My Shadow, and Me."—*Song title*
originally recorded by Frank Sinatra

Even though Adler and Jung moved away from Freudian doctrine and evolved their own techniques, this chapter uses the upper right quadrant in the therapeutic orientation model as a frame of reference to discuss the approaches of Freud and his break-away one-time disciples. Their theoretical base, intervention strategies, and the application of their processes to OD and OT practice will be examined. We begin with the "Me" in Sinatra's song: Freud and dynamic theory.

Dynamic Theory: Deterministic and Insightful (Upper Right Quadrant)

The central figure in the psychoanalytic movement was Sigmund Freud. His theory impacted not only psychotherapy, but also "art, religion, social organization, child development and education" (Arlow 1979 1). Although Freud's influence on the practitioner is primarily through other classically trained psychoanalysts—such as Adler, Jung, Rogers and Perls—who moved away from traditional Freudian analysis, it is important for the practitioner to understand the framework of his theory and intervention process.

THE FIVE PERSPECTIVES OF DYNAMIC THEORY

Topographical. To the Freudian, there are three different regions of mental activity: the preconscious (not immediately accessible but available), the unconscious (not accessible) and the conscious.

Structural. The personality is organized into three pieces: the id, the ego, and the super-ego. The id utilizes the pleasure principle. It wants what it wants and it wants it now! The ego evolves over time and develops from the id. Its function is to mediate between the id and external reality. The super-ego is that part of the personality that operates on the non-pleasure principle: if it feels good there must be something wrong. A former analyst colleague gives it a binary vocabulary: "should," and "should not."

Economic. We have a limited supply of "psychic" energy. For purposes of carrying on the species this energy is initially invested in the id. The process of investing this energy is what Freudian analysts call cathexis.

Dynamic. Energy is dynamic: it exerts a force and can move. Just as we go through the process of investing it through cathexis, we can undergo counter-cathexis and block. Through ego defense mechanisms, these blockages are channeled into the unconscious.

Genetic. This is Freud's developmental model, made up of the oral, anal, phallic, and latent phases (Arlow 1979). According to Freud we make bad bargains with ourselves early in life when we repress what happens during the phallic stage and cause the Oedipal or the Electra complex. The ego drives the causes of these complexes into the unconscious and we are in a state of dynamic stress which makes us neurotic.

FREUD'S INTERVENTION STRATEGY

The dynamic, to use an OD phrase, "change strategy," is to facilitate a "transference" (Arlow 21) in which the client projects their neurosis and early childhood difficulties that usually involve the parent, to the therapist. Transference is actively encouraged and insights are sought through "free-association." The ending portion is called "working-through" where the client uses her rational capacity to both end the transference, and de-cathexis their limited supply of dynamic energy.

LESSONS FOR THE PRACTITIONER

The concept of the preconscious mind. Freud's topographical notion of an area of consciousness that is blocked but accessible under the right circumstances is familiar to the practitioner who helps coaching clients access blind spots and see themselves as others see them. Practitioners don't encourage transferences or engage in a free-associative process to remove perceptual blockages. They use feedback, direct observation, and interactive dialog, but their goal is to help clients gain a clearer understanding of their impact on others (valid data), give them the opportunity to change (free choice) and help them make changes (internal commitment).

Awareness of transference. When a client tells a coach that, unlike him, she "lives in the real world," or defensively argues with the practitioner over the validity of objective data, or inappropriately and out of context tells the practitioner that he is wonderfully supportive and nurturing, there is transference in the air. The best coaches find ways to "go with the flow," not get hooked positively or negatively, and help the client gain helpful insights and make better choices. It isn't exactly "working it through," and certainly doesn't involve an intentional "transfer neurosis," but at a consultation level of interaction, it helps the client.

A potential practitioner danger is counter-transference. This happens when the consultant responds to client transference by projecting his own feelings of frustration with hierarchy, bureaucracy and authority back at the client or colludes with the client in an artificial mutual state of admiration. This is a particular threat to the lone-wolf practitioner who is counter-dependent to power and control and/or needs client affirmation. Practitioner counter-transference can be internal where the practitioner keeps it inside and inauthentically goes through the motions of the consulting process, or it can be external where the practitioner either aggressively argues and engages with the client in a hostile manner or engages in mutual psychological stroking. Both reactions are not useful for either the client or the practitioner. Gaining perspective by getting physical and psychical distance from the client, seeking help from a colleague, engaging in straight talk—if possible—with the client, or withdrawal from the consultation are optional courses of action.

Adler: The Platypus

Along with Jung, Adler was one of Freud's colleagues who, at least at one stage in his evolution, resided in the upper right quadrant of the model. A platypus is a small Australian animal that has a duck-like beak, a flat tail, lays eggs, and yet suckles its young. It is a little bit of everything, and Adler is sometimes described as a platypus because he defies categorization. He began as a psychodynamic analyst and moved toward a type of behaviorism. If he was starting his career today he would be a flag-waving leader in the organization transformation movement. He believed that a utopian society could be built only if people were transformed.

As a physician his early practice involved the treatment of trauma victims where he developed his theory of organ inferiority: people either compensated too little or too much from their injuries. Central to Adler's therapy were his concept of the inferiority complex and the compensating desire for power. Just as Freud emphasized repressed sex and aggressive drives as the prime forces in understanding human behavior and mental illness, Adler believed that the key factor was the quest for power as a result of the universal inferiority complex condition. His macro-social theory was a function of the maladaptation of inferiority. If people could be unburdened from the perception of individual inferiority, they would be free to channel their energy toward concern for other people.

ADLER'S INTERVENTION STRATEGY

Adler's strategy for facilitating change had two components. The first was to uncover the faulty lifestyle and help the person understand that they could choose to act as if they were not inferior. The second step was to replace the quest for power with a value reorientation: substitute striving for power with a desire for social action. Adlerian therapy is much more active than the Freudian variety (Mosak 1979). There is confrontation, discussion around value choices, and roleplaying, with the therapist giving both advice and encouragement. Adler's purpose was to help people change their belief systems and group therapy and educational processes were important components.

LESSONS FOR THE PRACTITIONER

Normative, re-educative transformational change. Many Adlerian techniques are directly applicable to the orientation of humanistic consultants, particularly OT practitioners. Group work, confrontation around value choices, normative re-educative belief system choices, and the channeling of people's negative feelings and dysfunctional behavior into a greater social good are central to an Adlerian practice.

Client responsibility. Unlike Freud's theoretical base and intervention strategy Adler's is a much more direct fit in the world of organization development and transformation. Freud was reductionistic—the individual was divided into parts—while Adler was holistic—the person's entire belief system was the subject of reorientation. Adler saw people as choosers and shapers of their own internal and external environments. Freud saw them as victims of early childhood traumas with implanted neuroses which could only be released through external intervention.

Gender equality. The humanistic value base of OD and OT promotes equality of all genders and sexual orientations. Adler, much ahead of his time, wrote that women were culturally undervalued and their roles needed reevaluation. Freud, however, said that women, "...because they envy men their penises—women are inferior—anatomy is destiny" (Mosak 1979 49).

Jung: The Mystic

The third one-time occupant of the upper right quadrant of the model is Carl Jung. If the three residents of that position: Freud, Adler, and Jung were alive today and working in the fields discussed in this book, we would see Freud as an organizational behavior professor at an empirically oriented university, reveling in theories and topologies. Adler would be a popular, robust figure in the organization transformation movement and Jung would be leading a semi-reclusive life, perhaps doing some writing and putting on highly experiential workshops with an intense, if narrow appeal.

Jung was much more mystical and spiritual than either Adler or Freud. If Freud's main theme was unconscious drives, and Adler's was power, Jung's was a quest for meaning. He was intrigued by common myths across disparate cultures which led to his theory of archetypes. Archetypes are found in the Jungian concept of the "collective unconscious."

JUNG'S INTERVENTION STRATEGY

For Jung, neurosis was caused by an inability to understand meaning and the way to discover that meaning was to communicate with archetypes through symbols. Kaufmann (1979 95) describes the related therapeutic process: "The therapist ... attempts to create, by means of a symbolic approach a dialectical relationship between consciousness and the unconscious ... a dialogue ... via dreams, fantasies and other unconscious products, between the conscious state and the patients personal as well as the collective unconscious."

Although classical Jungian analysis does utilize catharsis, dream interpretation, insight, and education—similar to those of Adler and Freud—the Jungian approach is differentiated by "individuation" and stage of life. Matoon (1981 235) writes:

> Transformation, or individuation, the stage in which the analyzed discovers and develops his or her unique individual pattern of life ... is the most specifically Jungian.... When the tasks of youth and early adulthood have been accomplished, a Jungian analysis is likely to center increasingly on archetypical images and the search for meaning.

LESSONS FOR THE PRACTITIONER

Foundation of the Meyers-Briggs Type Indicator. Practitioners of all varieties use the ubiquitous MBTI in their work. It's easy to obtain and fun to use. Although it suffers from a lack of defendable psychometric properties and is based on Jungian myth, not science, it seems to help managers understand and leverage their "type." Jung introduced the attitudes—extraversion and introversion—and the functions—sensation, intuition, thinking, and feeling. All are central components of the MBTI, but surprisingly some practitioner/users know little concerning their Jungian origins.

The yin and yang of gender traits. To Jung, male and female "traits" were opposite sides of the same coin. Practitioners dealing with polarities and their holistic integration can find much common ground in Jung's theory. As Matoon (1981 84) wrote, "Probably Jung's greatest contribution to female psychology is the concept of the animus, the contrasexual (male) archetypical component of the female psyche."

Legitimization of myth, mysticism, and spirituality. Jung's ideas of collective unconscious, meaningful coincidence (synchronicity), anama-animus, and the shadow, are both intriguing and illusive. One Jungian scholar friend who is now an organizational behavior professor says it is necessary to appreciate Jung like you appreciate a poem. Matoon (1981 xiii) agrees. She writes: "Academic psychologists have had little interest in Jung because he was as much a poet as scholar, and as much intuitive thinker as empiricist. His writing style has obscured his many creative contributions."

Humanistic practitioners, particularly those invested in individual and organization transformation have embraced the use of myth and spirituality and employ derivative concepts such as the "organizational unconscious." Humanistic coaches who help clients work through identity issues and decide how they want to work and what they want to do with their lives and careers are dealing, in Jungian terms, with "individuation."

Advice and Recommendations

- Although the language and concepts in Freud's genetic framework—phallic, oral, and anal stages and Oedipal or Electra complexes—seem far removed from the "real world" of business organizations, when considering the elusive nature of reality, the ubiquity of client preconscious blind spots, and the reality of coaching transference and counter-transference, Freud's theories are not all that far removed from today's organizations.
- The legacy of Freud's two dissident followers, Adler and Jung, directly impact the practitioner. Adler's focus on normative, re-educative change to build a better society and Jung's use of myth and symbol to tap into generic archetypes, are core components of many humanistic intervention strategies.
- A basic understanding of the relationship of the theoretical foundations of the big three to humanistic will benefit the practitioner, the operational manager, and the scholar/researcher.

12. A Discordant Quartet: Perls, Rogers, Ellis and Skinner

> "What one authority considers to be psychotherapy
> may be completely different from how other
> authorities see the process."—*Raymond Corsini*

We will now leave the big three to their posts in the deterministic-insightful quadrant and examine two therapies grounded in the humanistic value of free will (Gestalt and Person-Centered) and two on the deterministic side (Rational-Emotive and Behavioristic). Although different in approach, as Appelbaum (1993 422) reminds us all therapies have common objectives and "include elements of learning, feeling better, and behaving differently." Corsini (2000 2), however, addresses differentiating processes and therapeutic criteria: "What one authority considers to be psychotherapy may be completely different from how other authorities see the process." His report of a conference involving Rogers and Ellis (p. 9) reinforces this perspective:

> One of the most exciting meetings I ever attended included a major presentation by Carl Rogers on the necessary and sufficient conditions for psychotherapy. It was a most logical and impressive speech and it deeply affected me. However, the next speaker was Albert Ellis, who had been asked to comment on Roger's paper. Ellis stated that in 25 years of clinical experience he had many successful cases, but none of Roger's criteria seemed to him to be either necessary or sufficient.

Gestalt Approaches: Free Will and Action Orientation

The founder of gestalt therapy was Frederick (Fritz) Perls. According to a clinical psychologist colleague, Perls is to Jung what transactional analysis advocate Berne (1964), is to Freud. Berne popularized Freudian concepts and took much of the complexity out of dynamic theory through his concept of transactional analysis (TA). To say that Perls' approach is a popularized paperback edition of Jung in the same way that TA is a popularization of Freud, wasn't fair of my colleague. Gestalt psychology doesn't enjoy the same "pop-psych" relationship to Jungian theory as "parent—adult—child" have to their Freudian predecessors: id—ego—superego, and differs contextually and philosophically from Jung's approach.

Philosophy preceded psychology and the roots of gestalt psychology can be found in Hegel's dialectical process. This philosophy of contrast and syntheses is described by Durant (1953 295): "Of all relations, the most universal is that of contrast or opposition. Every condition of thought or of things—every idea in every situation of the world—leads irresistibly to its opposite, and then unites with it to form a higher or more complex whole." The gestalt theory of disorder deals with a painful polarization. If the thesis and its opposite antithesis don't come together in a holistic synthesis, there is a blockage and the patient/client is left with an unresolved polarization.

Gestalt Intervention Strategy

The theory of change is to "provoke awareness" by calling attention to incongruities between verbal and nonverbal behavior and focusing client awareness to what they are doing at the moment within their own phenomological field. Help is made possible by stimulating awareness and, according to the theory, with awareness, synthesis automatically follows (Simkin 1979). In this regard, gestalt treatment is different than most therapies. Others have a theory of disorder, a theory of change, and a set of procedures that "help" the client. In gestalt therapy, the theory of change—provoking awareness—is also the change procedure because, in gestalt theory, once awareness materializes, synthesis is automatic. "Provoking" methods include nonverbal communication, movement, and "here and now" interactions. External behavioral explanations are not used. Simkin (1979 273) explains: "The focus in Gestalt therapy is on immediate present awareness of one's experience. Cognitive explanations or interpretations of 'causes' or 'purposes' are rejected."

Dialogue and group work are routes to awareness. Appelbaum (1993 476) gives examples of how dialogue is used to "provoke" awareness: "The gestalt therapists in their pursuit of the here-and-now of experience say such thing as, 'talk to your long dead relative now,' 'Say how you feel now,'

'Act it, be it now,' 'Use the present tense.'" To a gestalt therapist, clients are in conflict between what should be and what is: the "painful" polarization. By facilitating awareness a spontaneous "aha" gestalt occurs.

LESSONS FOR THE PRACTITIONER

Working to discover and integrate polarities. Practitioners who focus on polarities and help clients integrate and learn from them are using undiluted gestalt technique. The theme of a past OD network national convention was "Integrating Polarities."

Confrontation and here-and-now learning. Practitioners who use direct confrontation interventions, those who tend to focus on nonverbal behavior, and group trainers who give here-and-now behavioral feedback are working from a gestalt frame of reference.

A phenomenological and existential orientation. Practitioners who are skilled at focusing on the act and the emotion as they are experienced, both in themselves and their client, are operating in congruence with gestalt theory. The ability to share who one is in the moment and be "with" the client without preplanned scripts or defined outcomes is the essence of a phenomenological helping relationship.

Internal and external awareness and integration. The practitioner striving to be authentic with her clients must also strive for achieving an internal gestalt. An early articulation of this process both for practitioners and managers is found in a book with the appropriate title, *Authentic Management: A Gestalt Orientation to Organizations and their Development* (Herman and Korenich 1977), that directly connects gestalt concepts to organization development.

Person-Centered Therapy: Free Will and Insightfulness

The name evolved from "non-directive," to "client-centered," to its current version of "person-centered" and is associated with its founder, Carl Rogers. Rogers was well known among the humanistic practitioners of the 1960s and 1970s as a writer, thought leader, and guru in the human potential movement. He was a faculty member at several Midwestern universities before joining the Western Behavioral Sciences Institute in LaJolla in 1963.

PERSON-CENTERED INTERVENTION STRATEGY

Roger's change strategy involved three conditions (Rogers 1957): unconditional positive regard, genuineness, and empathy. If the therapist behaved in congruence with these three conditions, client change would occur. This strategy is supported by his theory of disorder—a blocked socialization process that stifles self-actualization (Rogers 1961). To Rogers, applying "conditions of worth" to the granting of positive regard results in client anxiety.

His therapy sessions were very reflective, always safe and secure, and often filled with pauses and silence. In a transcript of one session (Meador and Rogers 1979 154) there were silences of up to 14 minutes and Rogers writes, "I believe that a word count would show that the client uttered little more than 50 words in the first of these interviews."

LESSONS FOR THE PRACTITIONER

Humanistic change model. Person-centered therapy with its orientation toward a non-judgmental, client-focused approach is congruent with humanistic practice. Rogers was considered a prototypical humanist and his change model supports that description.

Free choice orientation. Not applying "conditions of worth" and avoiding external prescription and judgment is consistent with humanistic values.

Focus on systemic transformation. Rogers's later work in educational reform and learner-centered teaching supports the social humanistic organization transformation movement.

Rational-Emotive Therapy: Deterministic and Action Orientation

Although located on the deterministic side of the therapeutic orientation model, rational-emotive therapy (RET), because of its cognitive, specific, action orientation, is the foundation of many practitioner interventions. Developed by clinical psychologist Albert Ellis, RET processes seem more "user friendly," and have a better fit in business organizations than other therapeutic interventions.

The premise of RET is that people's dysfunctional behavior is based on the way they construct their beliefs, construe meanings, and are driven by unreasonable "oughts" and "shoulds" (Ellis 2001).

RET INTERVENTION STRATEGY

RET therapists use a wide range of techniques—cognitive, emotion evoking, dramatic, and persuasive—to help clients come to grips with and drop self-defeating beliefs, emotions, and behaviors. They (Ellis 1979 206) "mainly employ a fairly rapid-fire active-directive persuasive-philosophic methodology. In most instances they quickly pin the client down to a few basic irrational ideas."

LESSONS FOR THE PRACTITIONER

Gets down to business with no theoretical foreplay. In the short-term, what-can-you-do-for-me-now, business world, RET cuts to the quick. In Ellis' (1979 205) own words:

> Rational-emotive therapists generally do not spend a great deal of time listening to the client's history, encouraging long tales of woes, sympathetically getting in tune with emotionalizing, or carefully and incisively reflecting feelings ... they consider most long-winded monologues of this nature a form of indulgence therapy, in which the client may be helped to *feel* better but is rarely aided in *getting* better.

Is compatible with two thirds of Argyris' (1970) humanistic intervention model. The RET model relentlessly confronts the client with valid data that contradicts her inappropriate belief system. Through behavioral rehearsal and roleplaying, it facilitates internal commitment.

Tends to violate the concept of free choice. RET is a powerful persuasive process. For the humanistic practitioner it becomes a value choice of ends and means. Is the cessation of dysfunctional emotions, beliefs, and behavior worth the price? When does persuasion evolve to coercion?

Is a direct foundation for coaching interventions. Roleplaying, all forms of feedback, practitioner-client dialogue, behavioral rehearsal, and group and individual process consultation, are all found in RET practice.

Behavioral Approaches: Deterministic and Action Orientation

Sharing the lower right quadrant of the model with RET are two less humanistically compatible cousins: behavioral therapy based on the contributions of Joseph Wolpe (1973) and behavior modification arising from the work of B.F. Skinner (1953). Wolpe's approach is a direct descendent of

Pavlov's classical conditioning and Skinner's orientation is toward operant rewards and punishments. There is a great deal of overlap between the two approaches and ... "the most comprehensive approach combines techniques from both schools" (Chambless and Goldstein 1979 231).

Behavioral interventions grew out of academic research by psychologists unlike the medical and clinical origins of other forms of therapy. Consequently observable and quantifiable behavior is what is valued. Some fundamentalists—"radical behaviorists"—discount anything that is not observable such as needs, drives, thoughts, and feelings. Others are somewhat softer and can discuss "inferred states."

BEHAVIORISTIC INTERVENTION STRATEGY

Behavioral therapy uses a variety of techniques including derivations of common reinforcement tools: positive, negative, punishment, and shaping. Other approaches use the concept of "corrective learning" (Chambless and Goldstein 1979) that employ systematic desensitization, flooding, and aversive encounters.

LESSONS FOR THE PRACTITIONER

A clash of values. So-called "radical" behaviorism that discounts feelings, needs, and drives and only values measurable, observed behavior is incompatible with humanistic values. Applying conditioning to human spirit and free will is not something a humanistic practitioner would do.

The paradox of effectiveness. Early reports that classical conditioning and behavior modification seemed to work in organizational environments (Luthans and Kreitner 1975; Connellan 1978) are valid today. Research is clear that under the right conditions, conditioning produces results. The reflective practitioner has the burden of honoring her values while knowing that behavioristic approaches can be effective.

The Influence of Therapeutic Approaches on the Practitioner

The four therapeutic approaches outlined in this chapter, when combined with the big three in the previous chapter, demonstrate their considerable impact on practitioners' strategies toward helping clients. This influence is depicted in Figure 12.

Figure 12

Influence of therapeutic approaches on the practitioner

THERAPEUTIC APPROACH	PRACTITIONER INFLUENCE
Freud (Dynamic Theory)	• **Illuminating blind spots** • **Understanding client transference** • **Avoiding practitioner countertransference**
Jung (Analytical Theory)	• **Meyers-Briggs factors (attitudes—introversion & extraversion; functions— sensation, intuition, thinking & feeling** • **Legitimization of myth and mysticism**
Adler (Individual Theory)	• **Transformational change for societal good** • **Clients as shapers of their own destinies** • **Gender equality**
Perls (Gestalt Theory)	• **Discovery and integration of polarities** • **Here-and-now orientation** • **phenomenological and existential focus**
Rodgers (Person Centered Theory)	• **Non-judgmental, client focused approach** • **Avoidance of external prescriptions** • **Learner-centered teaching**
Wolpe & Skinner (Behavioral Theory)	• **Value clash—radical behaviorism is incompatible with humanistic practice**

Advice and Recommendations

- One way to view humanistic therapists such as Rogers is as farmers: they plant a seed and whatever comes up was inherent within the seed, not applied from outside. They are non-deterministic, believing in free will and growth. The cure resides within the client: the therapist is a facilitator. Humanistic therapists and some of their heavily influenced practitioner-disciples, have faith that with the right conditions and help, the client will outgrow the problem. Rogers can be seen as a kindly farmer, careful not to step on the plant, setting up the growing conditions, then getting out of the way.

- Humanistic therapies were developed by people who saw themselves primarily as helpers and secondarily as scientists. In contrast, theorists such as Freud saw themselves as scientists and, because of circumstances, began to apply their science to helping.
- If humanists can be viewed as farmers, dynamic and behavioristic therapists can be seen as architects who design from a plan and restructure to fit it. Behaviorists start with a vacant lot and shape it. Dynamic therapists approach their architecture in the context of urban renewal: they tear down the old structures first, then rebuild them.
- In *Star Trek* terms, Spock would be a behaviorist and Captain Kirk would be a humanist.
- Perls and Ellis could be viewed in *Star Wars* terms. They seem to know more than they are letting on and the client is not sure she is safe. They are always making her confront things she may not want to know. Like Yoda who made Luke Skywalker confront his dark side, they push the client into self-revealing insights.

13. The Existential Influence

"As far as men go, it is not what they are that interests me,
but what they can become."—*Jean-Paul Sartre*

Just as many of the practitioner's interventions are popularized—some might even call them "dumbed-down"—versions of therapeutic techniques, humanistic practice also has roots in that branch of philosophy that deals with our purpose and need to create our own meaning for life: existentialism. Similar to the practice of using therapeutic-like interventions without an awareness of their origin, many practitioners are not aware of the existential grounding of their approach to helping.

Argyris, Meet Kierkegaard: The Existential Complexities of Valid Data, Free Choice and Internal Commitment

A basic tenet of existentialism is individual responsibility for *meaning making* and this individualism is reflected in differences between the approaches of the major names in the field: Kierkegaard, Nietzsche, Heidegger, Sartre, de Beauvoir, and Camus. There are, nonetheless, basic themes that link these philosophers together. The first is that life itself has no purpose or meaning, resulting in underlying alienation, anxiety, and forlornness. The cure is never external, through science or philosophy. The answer is internal. It's up to each individual, knowing they are trapped in a meaningless existence and facing the certainty of death, to make sense-making choices and lead an authentic and engaged life based on these choices.

These themes—death, meaninglessness, alienation, anxiety, and individual responsibility for creating meaning—are not the topics discussed around corporate boardrooms, coffee stations, or after-hours hangout bars. Nor, unfortunately, are they discussed enough—if at all—in gatherings of humanistic practitioners.

Existential Implications of Argyris' Model

Most practitioners ground their intervention strategy in Chris Argyris' (1970) classic three dimensional approach: valid data, free choice, internal commitment. To the existentialist, all three stages have profound implications. Each dimension is made more complex when viewed through existential lenses.

Valid data. To the existentialist, valid external data—data originating from a source outside the client's own individual meaning making—is an oxymoron. Each individual, if desiring to lead an authentic life, creates their own meaning, and valid data, therefore, is relevant and makes sense in a meaningless world only to the person receiving it, not the person giving it. The odds are very slim that the practitioner will be giving psychometric feedback to a lock-step disciple of Heidegger or Camus, or explaining 360 interview data to ardent followers of Sartre or Kierkegaard. She will, however, be working with a human who, in an existential context, is at some level of consciousness, trapped in an existence that only makes sense within his personally chosen meaning. In practical terms that doesn't diminish the value of feedback, it means that for it to be truly "valid data" it requires congruence with the client's internal sense of meaning. That's why giving useful feedback is an art, not a science.

Free choice. Sartre is famous for his phrase, "We are condemned to be free" (Panza and Gale 2008 167), and with that "condemnation" comes the responsibility of choice. Buckingham et al. (2011 271) capture Sartre's seriousness over this responsibility: "By making choices, we are creating a template for how we think a human life ought to be. Sartre writes, 'As far as men go it is not what they are that interests me, but what they can become.'" For the existentialist, freedom and choice are central to the necessary self-definition required to lead a responsible and meaningful life.

When practitioners give clients the freedom to choose, they aren't simply giving them a set of multiple choice–like options over how to deal with others' perceptions, they are asking them to complete a subjective, open-ended essay on how to lead their lives. Rather than force clients to make choices based on objective behavioral options, practitioners need to help them go deeper and examine what kind of person they are and what they want to become. Too many practitioners cheapen the value of a coaching relationship by presenting only shallow, one-dimensional behavioral options.

Internal commitment. To the existentialist Nietzsche, internal commitment means commitment to individualism. Writing of Nietzsche's concept of commitment Panza and Gale (2008 236) state:

> One thing is clear: if your way of engaging with the world isn't an expression of your own unique individuality, you're not in control of your own life. Knowing when you've been deceived is important, so living as an individual begins with understanding yourself, which Nietzsche suggests we're not terribly good at. Living as an individual requires the following:
> - Engaging with the world in a way that expresses your unique self.
> - Living self-critically to control elements of yourself that aren't reflective of you.
> - Being honest about the self at all times and avoiding deceptions.

For the responsible practitioner, internal commitment is much more than simply helping the client sign off on and agree to meet a series of externally imposed goals or objectives. It involves the much deeper task of helping the client discover and embrace his unique individualism.

The Humanistic Leap of Faith

Søren Kierkegaard, generally recognized as the founder of existentialism, was a "religious existentialist" and to become one required an against-the-existential-philosophic-grain leap of faith. Panza and Gale (2008 203) describe this leap:

> Although this stance isn't shared by all the existentialists, for Kierkegaard only an embrace of religious faith can avert false attempts to hide from anxiety or from the task of being a self. True passion, commitment, and risk can be found only in a leap of faith that embraces the aspects of your existence that you can't in any way rationally understand.

Theologian Paul Tillich (1952 190) frames the fundamental paradoxical concept in the words of his aptly titled book *The Courage to Be*: "The courage to be is rooted in the God who appears when God has disappeared in the anxiety of doubt."

Chapter 2 describes Weisbord's (1977) frustrating search for an OD definition and eventual conclusion that it could best be understood as a secular religion. That's an intriguing perspective, but one of uncertain validity. However, taking the notion of OD as a faith-based calling further, it can be argued that the authentic humanistic practitioner requires a leap similar to that described by Kierkegaard and courage, not unlike Tillich's, to fully embrace the principles and values of humanism.

While I think that some practitioners slide rather than leap into their profession, I also believe that at a deeper level, all authentic practitioners make a conscious choice. From an existential perspective, the result of that choice is engagement and passion, and from that passion comes power and a deep impact on clients. That passion and engagement is the hallmark of the best practitioners. When describing Kierkegaard's conception of passion Panza and Gale (2008 131) write: "Kierkegaard introduces a new notion of truth, one that differs from the typically accepted scientific version. To live truly and passionately, you have to embody your life's purpose and let it transform who you are." It is transformed, passionate practitioners who make lasting impacts on organizations and individuals.

The Necessary Price of Marginality

In order to be effective, practitioners must have values, skills, and perspectives that are unique enough for them to add value. By being different and passionately using that difference to help organizations develop and individuals to grow, practitioners operate outside the main stream culture of their clients.

LONELINESS, ISOLATION AND POTENTIAL BURN OUT

Isolation and loneliness is a recurring theme in existential literature and it is a constant environmental factor for the practitioner. In his address to the OD division of Academy of Management Porter (1978 2) stated the hazard of this necessary marginally. He describes practitioners as "people—people who use themselves as tools and thus have a tendency to grow rusty, blunt (or over-sharp), or burn-out." It is an absolute necessity for humanistic practitioners to give themselves a time out to recharge their batteries, clear their heads, preserve their passion, and commune with other practitioners.

MEMBERSHIP IN AN ARMY OF OUTSIDERS

It is cause for thought and perhaps concern that those who possess the majority of the skills needed to help transform organizations reap a minority of society's rewards. The practitioners who bring process skills, values related to participation and power-sharing and possess the necessary marginality, are disproportionately comprised of society's oppressed.

Lewin was looking back at the horror of what happened to Europe's Jews and searching for ways to bring change, dialogue, and processes that would provide alternatives to the obscene inhumanity and cruelty all too common in our species. A significant percentage of today's practitioners are made up of women, people of color, those who have been wounded, failed, or because of value conflicts, dropped out of organizational hierarchies. Some never entered the world of formal organizations because of predisposed attitudes toward business and competition. Some were drawn to organization development to grind their own axes, rectify their perceptions of "wrong" and change organizations according to their own, often retaliatory models.

The personal ax grinders don't remain in the field long. Again, an existential precept provides an explanation. In order to find purpose in a meaningless world, it is necessary to make a choice and pursue it with passion. Humanistic practitioners chose the pursuit of a helping, not a revenge-focused relationship: a role of other, not self, orientation. The market quickly sorts out the ax grinders from the helpers. Those in it for themselves, not for the clients, don't last long. The practitioner population that remains is made up of people who buy into a humanistic helping relationship and pursue it with existential passion. Many of these practitioners are outsiders who through ethnicity, gender, or belief systems, are different from most they attempt to help.

DEPRECATORY LABELING

Practitioners, particularly the internal variety, are not second-class citizens, but some who feel their values and cultural assumptions threatened, tend to dismiss their relevance. A prime example is the familiar labeling of the practitioner as one who resides in a world of unreality.

The defensive myth of the unreal world. This common form of labeling is usually stated in a condescending or pompous tone as, "That's interesting, but I live in the *real world*." One can fill in multiple reasons such as, "I don't have ... time ... energy ... or the inclination ... to think like you or engage in a dialogue.... I live in the real world." It is a myth because it places the practitioner in a place in the universe that doesn't exist. It's a projective form of defensiveness because it deflects the client's refusal to think outside of the box or acknowledge the existence of new paradigms reflected in the practitioner's "different" belief system.

When confronted by this form of resistance, the practitioner has the task of helping the client understand that, in an existential sense, we each define our own reality. I have found that, as with all forms of resistance, the most effective response is to bend like a willow—not counter-resist and break like a rigid oak. The best strategy is to name the resistance and have the patience to engage in a dialogue that helps the client understand that we all define our own reality; that we need to build on, cherish, and nurture our differences, not relegate them to a mythical kingdom in the land of unreality. Innovation, personal growth, and creativity are all closet dwellers in that unreal world. They are fragile and people working in these areas are unsure of their ground and highly susceptible to criticism. Given enough time and blessed with a reasonable client, I eventually ask them to speculate as to the number of creative thoughts and innovative ideas are never born, victims of an abortion caused by the "I live in the real world" put-down.

A Story of a Marginal Chief Executive

Top managers, too, can have values and approaches that are marginal. In those cases, their marginality can be in opposition to shareholders, business analysts, and some of their own team members. Such was the case of William Norris, CEO and Chairman of Control Data Corporation.

THE RISE AND FALL OF A HUMANISTIC CEO AND HIS COMPANY

The saga of William Norris and the company he founded, Control Data, is an important story that has not been fully told. The company that imploded in 1992 grew from less than 50 employees to over 60,000 worldwide with sales of $4.5 billion. Its raise and fall followed the paths of a long list of other mainframe and minicomputer firms: Honeywell, Burroughs, NCR, DEC, Wang, Data General and others. What was unique about Control Data was the humanistic marginality of Norris. His ideas concerning the role of business in addressing social issues were clearly in opposition to other corporate leaders and shareholder analysts. This perspective was illuminated in 1989 interview comments by Norris (Jensen 2013 259):

As I look across the land today, I see an education system that has gone to hell, bulging prisons, millions of Americans without health insurance, and a widening gap between the haves and have-nots. It is clear that the current lean-and-mean corporate mentality will assure further deterioration of our society. Corporations must address our unmet or poorly met needs as long range profitable business opportunities, in cooperation with government and other sectors. That is the only way that we will achieve a fair measure of social justice for all Americans.

William Norris backed his words with actions. Control Data started plants in inner-city locations and threw away rigid hiring standards. It invested in mobile health care units on a large American Indian reservation. It started adult literacy centers using computer-based education and found jobs for its graduates. Control Data worked with prison inmates, providing education and automobiles for released inmates needing transportation for jobs. Internally, Control Data pioneered a number of human resource innovations such as wellness promotion, drug and alcohol abuse help and several types of employee assistance programs. Norris believed in the power of small business and Control Data had processes to help employees finance and start small businesses.

Unfortunately, Norris' marginal, humanistic approach took place against a background of unprecedented competition and change in the U.S. computer business. Critics blamed his social programs for Control Data's demise but they were a very minor part of the corporation's activities. His transformational efforts faced heavy "not living in the real world," criticism as evidenced by this newspaper quotation (Lenberg 1985 A-4):

Corporate raider Irwin Jacobs said it is time for William Norris to leave his post as Chairman and Chief Executive Officer of troubled Control Date Corporation. "The best thing that could happen to Norris is a corporate raider would come and take over the company." Jacobs added, "Control Data prides itself on using corporate resources to delve into social issues such as poverty, education, and economic development. These programs have absolutely no benefit for the shareholders of Control Data." Asked to respond, Norris provided this statement. "I am more convinced than ever that the Control Data way of doing business will be perceived to be the correct one in the years ahead. In other words, Control Data and I personally are happy to be judged by history. I wonder what history's judgment of Mr. Jacobs will be?"

As head of an internal consulting division, I knew and respected William Norris. Judging from the demise of Control Data, Jacobs may have won a battle, but in the context of the necessary corporate transformational efforts in today's world, Norris may yet win the war. A remark Norris made, one that didn't make the papers and provides advice to marginal organizational leaders working to transform organizations, to a group of senior managers was a cogent, "Don't let the bastards grind you down!"

Advice and Recommendations

- Although many practitioners are not aware of it, there is a direct connection between humanistic practice and existential philosophy. A basic principle of existentialism is that we live in a meaningless world and it is the individual's central task to make his own meaning—discover a sense of purpose. Humanistic practice is grounded in free will—respecting the client's responsibility to make sense and choose what to do with the data and perspectives facilitated by the practitioner.

- The third leg of Argyris' intervention stool—internal commitment—when viewed through existential lenses, is grounded in the client's sense of personal meaning. Before making a commitment to change, the client has to have a clear view of "self," and that view is the result of individually derived purpose and meaning. If a client sees herself and the world as meaningless, any form of internal commitment will also be meaningless. The lesson for the practitioner is to never take the process of internal commitment lightly or mistake shallow, head-nodding agreement to an externally generated list of goals for true commitment. To secure true internal commitment, the practitioner must go deeper and help the client discover her own personal meaning and purpose. This requires patience, probing, asking the difficult but relevant questions, and sharing his own individual meaning.

- The most effective practitioners have found meaning in humanistic consultation. They have, as articulated by Kierkegaard, channeled that meaning into passion and used that passion to transform themselves. They have used their passionate, transformed meaning as a powerful tool to help individuals and organizations. Conversely, without meaning-fueled passion, it is not possible to perform as a humanistic practitioner.

- As evidenced by the demise of Control Data and its CEO, William Norris, leading a self-derived, marginal meaningful life, is not without derision and setbacks. Humanistic practitioners need the inner-resilience Norris plainly advocated when he told his colleagues to not "let the bustards grind you down." Martin Luther King framed it more elegantly and conceptualized marginality as non-conformity when he said in a 1967 speech, "The hope of a secure and livable world lies with disciplined nonconformists, who are dedicated to justice, peace and brotherhood. The trailblazers in human, academic, scientific and religious freedom have always been nonconformists. In any cause that concerns the progress of mankind, put your faith in the nonconformist!"

PART THREE

PERSPECTIVES
AND OBSERVATIONS

"A new organizational reality is emerging on the current
competitive landscape that is having important,
and in some cases adverse, effects on people
at work."—*Growing, Kraft and Quick*

The chapters in this part examine the effect of the new reality described by Growing, Kraft and Quick (1998 xv) on humanistic practice by offering ideas, perspectives, and observations. The section begins with a review of the impact of ten somewhat heretical, deceptively simple, yet profound propositions. It concludes with observations of practitioner competencies that constitute the "right stuff." A self-assessment (Appendix C) aids in this effort.

Philosopher Georg Hegel's concept of thesis, antithesis, and synthesis is used as a frame of reference to examine changing managerial paradigms and their impact on the practitioner. The metaphor of the practitioner as a hired gun illustrates the dangers of staying with a client too long and the possibility of becoming trapped in a fraudulent role.

Strategies for practitioners to help break organizational codependence and nurture the development of organizational learning cultures are discussed and a chapter focusing on ways operational managers can cope with and leverage the new reality is included.

14. Reflections
and Heretical Realities

"Organizations don't develop, people develop."
—*Frustrated general manager*

Offering perspectives on the practice of organization development and transformation and the state of organizational behavior scholarship, this chapter postulates ten deceptively simple, somewhat heretical realities as a stimulus for reflection and reorientation.

Organization Development Perspective

Organization development has roots that reach back to the depression and the human devastation and trauma of World War II. People like Lippitt, Benne, Bradford, and Lewin had goals to use normative, re-educative change to make organizations more humanistic, people more self-aware, and the world a better place. Two primary processes, both data-based, came from these early efforts: the survey—feedback—diagnostic—intervention strategy, and the T-group which dealt with data generated within a group.

These seminal processes soon spawned a number of techniques. The early Addison-Wesley book series (Schein, Bennis and Beckhard 1969), greatly facilitated their dissemination. Here one could discover methodologies such as "process consultation," "interpersonal peacemaking," and "organizational diagnosis." OD pioneers such as Schein, Beckhard, Lawrence, Lorsh, Bennis, and Walton became accessible to the working practitioner through this series.

From these beginnings came a proliferation of technologies, structured instruments, and detailed prescriptions for small group exercises offered by organizations such as University Associates that made a business out of selling intervention tools and processes. Today there are structural interventions, large group interventions, team building interventions, transformational interventions, socio-technical interventions, and countless other techniques for facilitating organizational change (Rothwell, Stavros, and Sullivan 2016). All are facilitated by a broad spectrum of practitioners, ranging from individual home-based consultants, internal practitioners, affiliates of larger consulting firms, and moonlighting organizational behavior faculty. Little wonder that some practitioners, particularly those who remember simpler times, long for a less technique-bound profession.

Organizational Behavior Perspective

Organizational behavior has spread into a highly diffused patchwork of psychology, sociology, motivational, and leadership models and processes. Just as organization development has unfolded as a technique-bound practice, organizational behavior has become an umbrella term for researching and teaching loosely connected management and leadership processes. Just as some OD practitioners are longing for a simpler, more humanistically congruent focus, some OB researchers and educators are seeking a clearer and less fragmented definition of their field. Some seem confused as to what it is they are supposed to be teaching and others wonder, as did Vaill (1985) how what they teach relates to the practical world of students who leave the classroom and "go out there," wherever "there" is.

Organization Transformation Perspective

Organization transformation continues its struggle to clearly differentiate itself from organization development. The struggle within the struggle is whether the objective of the transformation is to improve the bottom line of business organizations or transform society. The struggle within the struggle within the struggle is the question of whether transforming business organizations and society are really the same thing.

The Practitioner as Artist, Integrator and Sense Maker

The notion that there is such a thing as a pure "behavioral science" in the context of humanistic practice is misleading. Aside from the perspective of the radical behaviorists, OD and OT are much more arts than science. In the academic world, organizational behavior scholars have managed to cobble together an unwieldy but loosely integrative framework that serves as a "sense maker" and keeps the field from imploding. In the practical world of non-academic organizations it is the OD practitioner who is the sense maker, the artist who wields the brush and mixes the colors. In the ever-expanding universe of techniques, instruments, and interventions, it is the practitioner who provides coherence. Without practitioner facilitation and sense making, clients would just hear random notes, no music. In order to maintain their perspective, remain focused on people and humanistic values and not become lost in a maze of techniques and bureaucratic abstractions, practitioners, along with their organizational behavior colleagues, need to reflect upon ten deceptively simple, and at first glance, heretical, realities.

Ten Deceptively Simple Heretical Realities

Organizations do not develop, people develop. I first heard this reality from a general manager who grew weary of hearing a well-meaning but inexperienced organization development practitioner telling him the advantages of "developing his organization." What this executive really wanted was help in succession planning and leadership development. In a moment of frustration, he slapped his desk and made a pronouncement that forever changed that young practitioner's perspective on her work. "Organizations don't develop, people develop," he shouted.

He voiced a profound humbling reality. Organizations are not, in an existential sense, real. They are ideas, concepts, and shared abstractions. Thus, taken literally, organization development is not possible. What is possible is the development and nurturing of people with the propensity to bond with others, share common visions, and choose to work in collaboration for common goals.

Organizations cannot change because they do not really exist. Only people exist in an ontological "I am," sense. What can change are peoples' values, their alignment toward the goals of others, and their commitment to helping and empowering others.

Organizations cannot be transformed. Only people have that sense of "being" that we call spirit or soul. This can be ignited into a positive enabling force that can not only transform a person's sense of purpose, but can transcend the boundaries of time and space. Some believe it can transcend life itself.

Organizations do not behave. People behave. An organizational behavior class is, therefore, a class in people behavior within the shared abstractions we call an organizations.

Organizations are artificial systems. They are not real. When Weber defined "classical bureaucracy" he dealt with a philosophical abstraction. Some of his concepts: the separation of the office from the officer, a hierarchical flow of information and command, and the reduction of work into discreet elements were revolutionary in his time and are still useful, but they need to be understood in a philosophical context.

Managers are not homogenous entities. Management is a situational process. The manager of a fast food franchise in Iowa is very different than an upper middle manager in a London bank. Practitioners and theorists must stop conceptualizing managers generically and meet them within their respective cultures.

Practitioners are unique. There is no NTL type, feminist type, west coast type, or academic type. Each brings an individual set of skills, motivation, and vision into those abstractions called organizations and each has unique perspectives as to what constitutes change and transformation.

Theories and models are not the same as reality. People "are." They exist and must deal with death, freedom, isolation, and the creation of meaning. Theories and models are abstractions. They provide shared symbols and act as frames of reference, but they don't, in an ontological sense, exist.

Techniques are symbols and processes, not statements of facts. If a person's Meyers-Briggs type is designated as ENFP, she is not, in an existential sense, an extroverted intuitive with feeling. To say that is what she *is*, as opposed to how she filled out the instrument form, is too simple, too sterile, and too far from the uniqueness that underlies that person's humanity.

People are real. In order to understand them, help them, and consult with them, humanistic practitioners need to experience them individually, personally, and undiluted and unfiltered by theories and abstractions. As much as they are tempted to experience others in the abstract, they must interact with them within a unique phenomenological horizon.

Advice and Recommendations

- The raw material in humanistic practice is people. It may seem elegant and sophisticated to conceptualize practice in a framework of models, theories, and abstractions, but doing so is at best a distracting diversion and is always a barrier to the creation of an authentic helping relationship.

- It is a professional hazard to use our theories and models as shorthand for the uniqueness of our clients. Practitioners need to continually guard against only seeing clients as an extensions of our theories.

- It is easy for either the consultant practitioner or the humanistic line manager to, in the heat of battle, get bogged down in the intricacies of an intervention and lose sight of the client as a unique individual.

- It is very useful to use the ten realities as a frame of reference to engage in a dialogue with a colleague. I have also found that discussing the realities in a group setting with other practitioners promotes a very productive discussion of intervention strategies, tools, and untested assumptions.

- When stuck or frustrated, I have found that backing away and letting intuition and the client guide the process is nearly always more productive than rigidly adhering to a theory or model.

15. Six Managerial Paradigms in the Process of Becoming

"Each stage of world-history is a necessary moment in the idea of the world spirit."—*Georg Hegel*

Philosopher Georg Hegel saw history as a path to a single unifying whole, what he called "world spirit." The method of moving along that path involved the dialectic process "every notion or 'thesis' contains within itself contradiction or 'antithesis,' which is only resolved by the emergence of a newer, richer notion, called a 'synthesis'" (Buckingham et al. 2011 182). Another way to look at a change in world view is what Thomas Kuhn (1996) described as a paradigm shift.

This sense of movement can be viewed from three points of reference: what was, what is, and what is in the process of becoming. Using Hegel's concept of thesis, antithesis, and synthesis, one can see an old paradigm, its opposite, and a new syntheses of the two. Figure 13 depicts this movement as six shifts in the evolution of humanistic management, which are described in this chapter.

From Management as a Science, to Management as an Art, Toward Management as a Craft

Behaviorists such as Skinner (1972) and Wolpe (1973) sought to formulate a management science based on the principles of conditioning. Earlier Taylor (1911) published his *The Principles of Scientific Management* in which humans were seen as machine-like components of the production process. Many of today's business schools are heavily oriented toward quantitative analysis and mathematical modeling.

Taylor's scientific management, behavioristic conditioning, and isolated

Figure 13

Managerial paradigm shifts viewed through a Hegelian lens

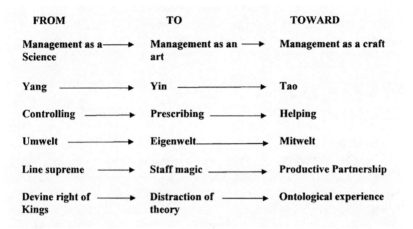

FROM	TO	TOWARD
Management as a Science	Management as an art	Management as a craft
Yang	Yin	Tao
Controlling	Prescribing	Helping
Umwelt	Eigenwelt	Mitwelt
Line supreme	Staff magic	Productive Partnership
Devine right of Kings	Distraction of theory	Ontological experience

statistical analysis had little to do with the issues faced by real managers in unique, situational environments and a new way of perceiving management began to emerge that was more compatible with humanistic principles. The process of management began to be perceived as an art. Vaill (1989) captured the trend in his aptly titled book, *Management as a Performing Art.*

No longer were there scientifically proven principles or elaborate analytical processes that spewed out hard data leading to the one "right" decision. The manager was intuitive, charismatic, making decisions and motivating people based on feeling, intuition, and orchestration. This artistic process is much closer to what actually happens in organizations and is appealing to those—new, entry-level, millennial managers—rebelling against the stilted concept of scientific management, the manipulation of behaviorism, and the oppression of mindless mathematical models. It, however, is not the way relevant, humanistic managers function. The notion of management as a freelancing, intuitive, creative process is a quasi-narcissistic process, discounts necessary external data, and does not place the manager in a helping relationship.

The relevant manager of the future will be a hybrid and practice the craft of management. She will cobble together traditional management functions (hard data-driven decisions and strategic focus) with humanistic helping skills. This cobbling process will constitute the *craft* of management.

The effective practitioner of the craft of management must have a high degree of emotional intelligence, be self-aware, have interpersonal competence, and possess group process skills. These are the attributes of a competent helper, be she therapist, counselor, or manager. These skills are more scientific than found in an intuitive artist and more spontaneous and less reliant on positivistic proof than found in a management scientist.

From Yang, to Yin, Toward Tao

In oriental philosophy, the Tao is the way. Fritjof (1984 24) describes the meaning: "Complete, all encompassing, the whole. These names are different, but the reality sought in them is the same, referring one thing ... it is an ultimate reality which underlies and unifies the multiple things and events we observe." In humanistic practice, the idea is manifested in ways such as movement from left-brain dominance to right-brain processing, toward what Ned Herrmann (1995) calls "whole brain." It is the blending of masculine and feminine to a unifying androgyny.

The shift from Yang to Yin involves moving from a hard, dominant, analytical orientation to a softer, yielding, supporting orientation. Early management was Yang management. It was non-supportive and prescriptive. A more humanistic approach, Yin, emerged that was more open, trusting, and participative. This approach, although congruent with some humanistic values, if overdone can lead to an erosion of standards and lack of responsibility. The state of public education in the U.S. as reflected in science, math, and reading test scores is an example of overdone Yin.

What is emerging is more than a one-dimensional Yin or Yang approach. What is needed is the Tao, a combination that is more than both. When frustrated managers use the trite word, "synergy," they are really seeking the Tao. To be successful in transforming organizations, leaders need to be masculine and feminine, left-brain and right-brain, analytical and intuitive. They must be the best of both and more than both. The leaders of the future will follow the Tao.

From Controlling, to Prescribing, Toward Helping

The traditional definition of management (Fayol 1949) incorporates a number of "ings," as in controlling, evaluating, directing and planning.

What it lacks is the one "ing" that fits today's environment and a humanistic approach: helping.

When people are overly controlled, evaluated, and directed, the result is lowered productivity and an erosion of creativity. Some overly zealous advocates of McGregor's (1960) theory Y prescribe a total suspension of anything smacking of theory X management. Paradoxically, that prescription doesn't work either. When people are never controlled, evaluated, or held accountable, productivity also declines and unifying strategy erodes. In reality, there is no "best way" to manage, but there are many "best ways" being prescribed: management should always be participative; management should follow the Japanese model, be consensual and inferential; managers should "walk around"; managers should lead by "objectives." We live in an age of prescriptions with many books written and much money made from managerial "shoulds," and "oughts."

Humanistic practitioners are not without their own "shoulds." The relevant manager *should* be a helper and *should* possess a repertoire of helping skills. However, the application of these skills and what constitutes help is entirely situational and cannot be reduced to a formula. The manager of the future will be a situational helper. Even the most humanistic leader will need some degree of controlling and directing behaviors, but they will have the skills to frame those behaviors in a helping orientation.

From Umwelt, *to* Eigenwelt, *Toward* Mitwelt

These German words are used by May and Yalom (2000) when describing existential psychotherapy. *Umwelt* is the natural world that includes biological needs, drives and instincts. *Eigenwelt* is the way a person relates with himself. *Mitwelt* is the world of other people and community

They put into a sentence (p. 272), what I have come to believe is a problem with many newly converted humanistic managers: "How can we be sure that we are seeing the patient as he really is, or are we simply seeing a projection of our own theories about him?" One answer lies within a key concept in existential therapy: the "ontological" experience or the study of "being in the world." In order to do this, it is necessary to understand the unique world where the client exists and interacts.

In managerial terms, the most basic way of "being in the world" would be Umwelt. The Umwelt manager would exist at the lowest plane of Maslow's hierarchy and engage in exploitive and self-serving management.

Two examples would be the primitive slave master and self-serving politicians who, as the poet Matthew Arnold wrote (1867 86), would send "ignorant armies" to "clash by night."

The Mitwelt managerial mode emphasizes human relations skills. It is other orientated and based on compassion and the ability to transcend self-interest and have the capacity to love others. However, self-awareness and acceptance—Eigenwelt—is necessary in order to truly function at this level. As May and Yalom (2000 276) phrase it: "The importance of Eigenwelt was stressed by Friedrich Nietzsche and Søren Kierkegaard who continually insisted that to love presupposed that one must already have become the 'true' individual, the 'Solitary One,' the one who 'has comprehended the deep secret that also in loving another person one must be sufficient onto oneself.'"

In order to be truly relevant to the needs of employees, the manager must have an adequate sense of himself in all of his existential loneliness and differentiation. It isn't sufficient to simply be schooled in humanistic approaches. The manager/practitioner must develop a sense of Eigenwelt. Only then, can he use his humanistic Mitwelt skills to engage in authentic helping relationships.

From Line Supreme, to Staff Magic, Toward a Productive Partnership

"Line managers have the ultimate responsibility. Staff functions only exist to help line managers do their job better. Line managers should be paid more, enjoy higher status, and be the only ones promoted to senior executive positions because, after all, they bring in the money and have ultimate responsibility for the bottom line." This is a composite quotation based on my memory of the opinions of many managers over many years. These and similar sentiments were the cause of a structural inferiority complex for staff functions. This was reflected in the classic "line supreme" organization chart, with staff functions shown as appendages to the primary hierarchical, line triangle.

The information revolution changed things and the downsizing epidemics of the 1980s and 1990s accelerated the change. With the increasing complexity of organizational relationships, globalization of commerce, the growth of information technology, and the need for simultaneous information in all organizational corners, the concept of the line manager as the sole dispenser of information and power was blown away in one great burst of computing power.

All middle managers are endangered species, their communication link between the top and the bottom broken and replaced by personal computers. As product cycle times shortened and global competition accelerated, the best and the brightest new employees gravitated toward staff roles in marketing, information technology, accounting, supply chain management and, in some firms, human resources. The concept of a supreme line manager supported by narrow subservient staff specialists eroded. The new generation of specialists were better educated than their managers, found it easier to change jobs, were well paid, and had much more loyalty to their professions than to their employers. Suddenly, traditional line managers found themselves dependent on the new wave of staff specialists.

These specialists did do magic. Their computers projected trends, produced mathematical models, revealed customer profiles, and analyzed markets. HR specialists monitored compliance with the equal employment laws and occupational safety and health regulations. Lawyers facilitated mergers, and accountants cleverly manipulated the numbers and tax obligations. These talented staff members did such a good job and line managers spent so much time reading their reports, struggling to comprehend their jargon, and meeting with them, that they forgot to interact with "normal," working employees.

Simplistic though it may sound, "management by walking around" is a powerful concept. It requires the manager to step away from staff-centric interactions and experience employees in all of their phenomological uniqueness. Information and staff analysis are essential management tools, but analytical processes will never replace intuition and first-hand employee interaction with all of its rich, conflicting, and unanalyzable intricacies.

Never again will managers be able to be effective without relying on staff specialists; the world is too complex and technology too advanced. At the same time, line management and staff specialists must form a partnership based on mutual appreciation of the wonder and awesome potentialities of motivated people. If organization transformation is to occur, it will be vested in individual people rather than trend data. It will be facilitated by line and staff working as partners, neither ignoring staff technology, nor the need to touch the people.

From the Divine Right of Kings, to the Distraction of Theory, Toward the Ontological Experience

Until the Second World War, particularly in countries without the populist tradition of the U.S., but, also in cultural pockets of the U.S., management was based on the perceived God-given right of one class of people to lead another. Leaders were born, not made. Politicians had the unilateral right to order lesser mortals into battle to be killed. Kings were kings because God willed it. The managerial class had the right to exploit workers because their primary purpose was as a "thing," a necessary, dehumanized input into the profit equation.

The U.S. was not immune, nor has it yet completely escaped the divine right paradigm. If children were to be sent to coal mines to die before they reached their forties and women grew old in less than ten years from working at the looms; that's the way it was ordained. If factories were to be closed and leave entire towns without a source of employment or a center of self-esteem for their citizens, that was just the way the system worked: profit and shareholders dictated.

As the divine right paradigm began to wane and it became clearer that leaders were made, not born, academics and thoughtful managers began to articulate theories as to how leaders were "made," how employees should be motivated, and how organizations should be managed. We had theories X and Y; a Japanese variant, theory Z; employees were seen to be motivated by "the job itself," not by supportive "hygiene factors." Participation, self-actualization, and achievement were all billed as prime motivators. If one theory didn't work, there was always another around the corner. Countless managers attended innumerable seminars and workshops, spending lots of money and emerging with new theories of the "right way" to do it.

Mental health professionals joined the theory game. Behaviorists would condition employees to happiness. Dynamic theorists would help employees find happiness by achieving insight into repressed drives. Some like Bion would attribute Freudian concepts to group dynamics. Rogerians would emphasize empathy, unconditional regard and genuineness as a key to developing healthy, motivated, employees.

There is nothing inherently wrong with any of the management or mental health theories. Many are congruent with humanistic values. The problem is that they become distractions. We become trapped by the boundaries and projections of our theories. We can learn from the existentialists and begin to perceive managerial interactions through the lenses of what May and Yalom (2000 274) call the "I am" or the "ontological" experience: "The 'I am' experience, or the experience of being, is known in existential therapy as an *ontological* experience. This word comes from two Greek words, *ontis* meaning to be and *logical* meaning 'the science of,' Thus it is the 'science of being.'"

In order to be relevant to the transformational needs of organizations and individuals we need to see people their phenomenological uniqueness, not as projections of our theories. In order to see them this way, we need to see ourselves through ontological lenses—have an "I am" orientation— know who *we* are so we can connect with who *they* are.

The relevant practitioner/manager will not abandon theories and models (how else can they begin to make sense out of organizational complexity?) but they will not be a slave to them. They will have the ability to perceive people in a fresh phenomological horizon so that they and the person they are helping can interact while in the process of being, not as sterile and abstract extensions of each other's theory.

Advice and Recommendations

- If you are a manager/practitioner you have a difficult but exceptionally important role. If organizations are to transform both for the benefit of their shareholders and society, the transformation will happen through the efforts of managers, not external consultants. Humanistic consultants can be of great assistance, but only line management can make it happen.
- The paradigm shifts described in this chapter require a "letting go"—"holding on" response from transformation oriented managers. It will require courage to let go of the comfortable old and even more courage to embrace the unfamiliar new. It will help to find like-minded colleagues as both a support and value clarification group. It is very lonesome and usually ineffective to be a "lone ranger."
- If you are an OB or an OT practitioner, you have a twofold task. You must first examine your own paradigms and decide if your behavior and interventions support the shift to new ways of

135

"being." If you are able to walk the new talk, you can play a vital role in supporting your line manager clients as they struggle with the transition.

- If you are a researcher, student, or OB teacher, take the time to do an ontological inventory to be certain you have the perspective to make observations without them being extensions of a pre-conceived model or theory.

16. The Practitioner as a Hired Gun

"Have Gun Will Travel"—*Paladin's business card*

Have Gun—Will Travel was an exceptionally popular television series with Gene Roddenberry of future *Star Trek* fame among its stable of writers. Its primary character, Paladin, (based on the twelve Paladins—the foremost warriors in Charlemagne's court), was a well-educated hired gun who routinely left his culturally sophisticated life in San Francisco to do battle in the wild West. He tried to intervene in problems before resorting to violence and for those he deemed worthy and in need who couldn't afford his steep fee, he worked for free.

In many ways, Paladin was a consultant, closer to the traditional management consulting model, but with some humanistic traits. He sold his expertise—his fast gun—to clients (his traditional consulting orientation) but he first attempted to help clients (a humanistic trait) before drawing his weapon.

I once took a series of psychological tests as a part of a master's program in organization development. I was pleased and positively reinforced by most results but was troubled when told that, based on one instrument, I fit the profile of many helping professionals since I needed less empathy and affection than I showed or gave to my clients. In short, I apparently, along with others in the helping professions, was very good at faking it. The person giving me that feedback rejected my categorization of "faking it," and, instead said that it was healthy since helping professionals can't function well over time if they become too emotionally attached to their clients. A long discussion ensued and I concluded that OD consultants who fit that profile could slip into roles as actors or "hired guns," selling our empathy, compassion, and process skills to the highest bidder. He rejected that categorization too, but I left the session convinced that, but for our three-barreled weapon—valid data, free choice, and internal commitment—we weren't all that different from Paladin.

Parallels Between Practitioners and Gunslingers

LONE RANGERS

There are interesting parallels between practitioners and the gunslingers of the Old West. Many of the most successful practitioners, like their gunfighter antecedents, are, deep down, loners—individual contributors who bond with a small number of others, usually other practitioners. It's ironic that they excel in teaching group process skills and team dynamics, yet steer clear of group activities in their own lives.

As was the case with the fictional Paladin, they leave their home base, ride into town, do their thing, and ride off into the sunset—in their case they often use a 747, rather than a horse. Just as another fictional Western pair—the Lone Ranger and Tonto—rode away, with a "Hi-Ho Silver" and a "Get-em-up Scout," apparently unmoved by the profound impact they had on the lives of the people they helped in the town; the practitioner, after conjuring up intense feelings and interactions that linger in the hearts and minds of clients, flies off, aloof and alone, unable to share in the joy of what he has planted.

THE HIRED GUN CAN BECOME THE PROBLEM

In Western lore there are stories of the hired gun who is hired to clean up the town, accomplishing the task, but staying too long, accumulating power, and becoming the problem he was retained to solve. To illustrate I have one optimistic fantasy and one actual example.

The optimistic fantasy. A tall, morally rigid gunfighter is hired by the corrupt founding fathers of an Old West town to get rid of the outlaws. He does the job but stays to straighten out the founding fathers. The reason for optimism is that too many practitioners are retained by top management to facilitate transformational change but are limited by the same top managers from dealing with the central systemic issues. In this fantasy, the gunslinger/practitioner is able to move beyond the protective top management cultural barriers and fuel the fires that stimulate a transformation that includes the entire organization.

The actual example. Byron, a practitioner with a Ph.D. in counseling psychology was retained by the chief operating officer (COO) of a growing two thousand–person Florida-based technology firm. In past relationships with Byron, or "Dr. By," as he liked to be called, I found him to be hampered by a tendency toward self-promotion and a propensity to tell the client what the client wanted to hear, not what he needed to hear. I, and my colleagues thought Dr. By would have made a much better salesman than an OD practitioner because he was gifted at forming quick shallow relationships and, with a very limited repertoire of interventions, tended to intervene with little or no diagnosis. In the Florida firm, he contracted for a team building session that was reported as successful. The human resource director was functionally responsible for screening OD consultants but she let the COO choose for himself and, despite her bias for another candidate, he picked Byron.

A week after the session, she was surprised to run into Byron in the employee cafeteria. He told her that the COO had asked him to stay a bit longer and do some additional work. Rather than provoke a turf battle with the COO, she let it pass, thinking Dr. By would clear out in a few days. Two weeks later, she got a call from a real estate agent asking her to verify the fact that her firm would be paying for a six-month lease on an oceanfront apartment for Dr. By (It was September and Dr. By's home was in Minneapolis). Outraged, she discovered that the COO had put Byron on a six-month retainer and agreed to pay for an apartment. She went to their mutual boss, the president, to complain but was told that he had already met Dr. By and was very impressed with him, in fact Byron would be facilitating a team development session with his own staff which, of course, included her and the COO. I'd done some work with her in the past and she explained her situation to a colleague and I over dinner. Here is a paraphrase of what she said:

> I can't get him out. He's weaseled his way in and, if I push too hard, it will look like I'm threatened by him. The only thing I'm threatened about is that I don't trust him and have no confidence that he'll add any value to the president's quasi-dysfunctional team. Not only that, he has, without asking my permission, co-opted one of my junior staff members to help him. He's a young, impressionable new college hire and I don't want him misguided by Dr. By's seat-of-the-pants approach.

What she described was a perfect example of the OD equivalent of the gunfighter overstaying his welcome and becoming the problem himself. Our only advice was to keep her distance and wait for Dr. By's relationship with her firm to predictably unravel. It didn't take long. The COO fell out of love with Dr. By when he learned that he had disclosed some personal information to the president that Byron had assured him would be kept confidential. The parting episode was when the president's team building session was canceled after the first day. Dr. By had neglected to brief or get the president's buy-in for a feedback session from his direct reports. During the session Byron allowed a number of destructive and personal attacks to take place. Rather than go through the legal hoops necessary to cancel his retainer contract, the firm kept paying him but just didn't use him until the six months elapsed. They also didn't cancel the lease and Dr. By had a free oceanfront escape from the icy blasts of a Minnesota winter.

POTENTIAL TO BECOME TRAPPED
IN A FRAUDULENT ROLE

Gunfighters "made their bones" by putting notches on their guns when they were young, irresponsible, and caught up in the heat of battle. Like Frank and Jesse James, Butch Cassidy, and to some extent Clyde Barrow and Bonnie Parker, they—through age, wisdom, or physical decline—wanted to escape but found they were stuck in a role they no longer wanted to play. This sense of role entrapment also occurs in organization development and other fields where a loss of faith or a diminished sense of being "called" is a potential hazard. Again, I have a fantasy and an actual example as illustrations.

The fantasy. This fantasy was stimulated by a former Baptist missionary and preacher who is now an OD practitioner. A missionary, living among a self-contained tribe in a foreign culture has lost his faith. He goes through the motions of conversion and indoctrination because, without that there would be no point. A phony role seems better than no role at all. He can't connect with the tribal members he has converted because they have the faith he has lost. He can't pull up stakes and go back to the mission headquarters because they would either send him somewhere else or fire him. In either case, he'd be a loser. So, he's stuck; a problem to the tribe, he has nothing but fraud to give them, a problem to his mission, and most of all, a problem to himself. The non-fantasy tragedy is that there are, as illustrated in the following example, organization development practitioners trapped in similar untenable roles.

The example. Cindy started out as an external OD consultant employed by a boutique firm. Tired of getting low-level assignments and sharing her hourly billing rate with the firm, she left after eighteen months, hung out a shingle, and became an independent practitioner. She hit a wall that is shared by many who take this path: she had no problem delivering professional humanistic consultation, but she had a big problem finding clients. Frustrated and out of money, she accepted a job as an internal consultant with a Chicago-based division of a large multinational corporation. She thought it would be an ideal situation, the best of both worlds: a steady paycheck, job security, and an unlimited number of needy clients. She was wrong.

Her boss, a human resource administrator in the firm's New York headquarters hired her because his boss, the HR vice president, attended a T-group and thought it would be a good idea to put an OD professional in all the company's large divisions. There was no plan for what those people would actually do, no discretionary budget, and the administrator he put in charge had no conception of what OD meant or how it could help the firm. Cindy was left to flounder and she soon learned the true meaning of not being a prophet in one's own land.

After two years of false starts, rejections, inconsequential make-work tasks, and countless insults (the division supplied electronic components to the navy and many of their managers were ex-officers fluent in navy staff insults such as "staff-weenie," or "staff-puke"), Cindy stopped trying. She actually received a positive performance appraisal and a couple of hefty salary increases, which she used to help finance a lake front condo and a new car. Not only did she give up trying, but she gave up on the promise and potential of humanistic practice.

Similar to the stuck missionary in the fantasy, she was trapped in a fraudulent role. She didn't want to go back out on her own—she liked the salary and the security—and she had lost faith in the power of OD. Her story didn't have a happy ending. The firm lost their primary navy contract and she lost her job. The last I heard of her, she was working as a temporary administrative assistant and taking classes in accounting.

TENDENCY TO SELL THEIR SERVICES
TO THE HIGHEST BIDDER

It is a sad fact that those organizations who can afford to pay competent practitioners are often either the ones who need change the least, or those who are intrigued by the potential but only want to sample it as a toy. Practitioners are gunfighters wielding weapons of participation, choice, trust, and the potential for facilitating deep and abiding change, but many organizations tend to use them in the same way early entrepreneurs used social projects and corporate "giving." The old capital and land barons used manipulative, coercive, and exploitative people strategies to build their empires. Once they arrived they "got religion" and channeled a small portion of their gains into charitable projects and socially responsible giving. In the same way, some conservative, power-coercive organizations allow outside practitioners and internal humanistic managers to nibble away at the edges of their culture but find ways to deflect and block fundamental transformational change.

THE PROPENSITY TO CHOOSE
CLEAN, SOLVENT, TARGETS

Despite having a solid base in humanistic values, there are few Mother Theresas in the practitioner ranks. Most not only like to get paid for their gun-slinging, but prefer nice hotel conference rooms in the sunbelt to squalid slums or dangerous war zones. I attended an OD conference in San Diego held in a luxury hotel where seasoned practitioners spent nearly a week discussing OD, change, interventions, and the latest tools and techniques. Not fifty miles from our conference room were the slums, corruption, drug dealers, and human brutality in parts of Tijuana. While we were sleeping in our modern hotel rooms, entire families were living in shacks made out of refrigerator cartons and warped plywood. Why didn't we stop talking about tools and techniques and spend some of our time applying our humanistic values to dwellers of the slums in Tijuana? OD pioneer Bob Tannenbaum supplied a partial answer in a keynote speech to an OD network national conference (Van Endye, Hoy and Van Endye 1997 171):

> The narrow adherence to the tool kit by many in our field does trouble me deeply, for it is dehumanizing OD. If I were to characterize OD at present, I would say that is less humanistic than it was a few years ago; and I am concerned that the trend is in the direction of even less humanism. *People* are becoming less important to us, less central than issues such as "Can I run this kind of an exercise?" or "What is the latest method being used?"

Organizations that need the best practitioners have to offer are not characterized by the clean, air-conditioned corridors and soft-chaired conference rooms found in business organizations. They are most likely represented by the screaming, smelling, dangerous world of broken families and fractured political systems. A vast, demoralized horde of warped and brutalized people that could benefit from humanistic assistance. The reality is that the majority of practitioners seek payoff for their experience and education and, therefore, opt for facilitating change in organizational systems that reward them in economic, rather than social, currency.

THE DILEMMA OF CHOICE

The fictional Paladin chose which clients were worthy of his gun-slinging talents. If he lived today, he, along with contemporary practitioners, would have some difficult choices. It is not that easy for a practitioner to choose sides, to ride into a town—enter an organizational system—decide if the client is worthy of her services, and if not, simply ride away. Perhaps, as Paladin sometimes did, even change sides and join the client's enemy—in an OD business context, consult with the firm's competitor. Paladin wouldn't be a good fit as a practitioner in today's world. There are economic, social, political, and financial forces that influence the practitioner's decision of what organizations to help. They also have conditioned, sometimes unconscious, cultural and motivational gremlins that shape their actions.

Paladin's Choice and Practitioner Options

If Paladin had magically been transported to a neutral country during World War II, reincarnated into an OD practitioner, and given the option of helping either the German or U.S. air forces, his decision would not be as clear is it might seem. The strategy on both sides was to not be overly concerned with bombing civilians and it was the first war where large numbers of civilians were killed by bombs. Historians report that the English and American pilots were perhaps the most educated and intellectually liberal warriors in history. They were labeled as "nice boys." Should Paladin accept an assignment to train these "nice boys" so that they could drop their bombs more efficiently—enable them to kill more people? An option would be to simply ride away and wash his hands of any moral responsibility. Another choice would be to join the Germans and help their pilots kill more English civilians.

I think that Paladin, as a humanistic practitioner, would not ride away and escape a moral choice. He would pick the English and American side as the lesser of two evils. Then, after the war ended he would work with both sides to help develop systems and processes to avoid future repetitions.

All modern OD practitioners, to some degree, face Paladin's choice. They work for financial institutions that have been labeled greedy and manipulative, governments that seem more concerned with staying in power than helping people and private businesses that worship shareholder value and executive compensation at the expense of worker's security. With enough scrutiny, ugly, non-humanistic warts can be found in all organizations.

What are humanistic Paladins to do these days? They, as a few have tried, could form communes, drop out and beat their guns into plowshares—or in their case, their books, instruments, and structured interventions could be shredded and sold as fertilizer. They could become keynote speakers and join the "ed-u-tainment" lecture circuit, the modern equivalent of old-time gunfighters joining circus side shows or Wild Bill Hickok's Wild West Show. They could withdraw from active involvement, write books, or form academic units that study gun fighting.

I believe that the vast majority of humanistic practitioners will do none of these things. They will, along with the fictional Paladin, select the organizational equivalent of the least evil option. They will, as in the past, work for change within organizations by helping responsible operational managers keep the flickering hope of lasting transformation alive.

Advice and Recommendations

- The familiar Western tale of the outsider—the lone-wolf gunfighter who comes from out of town, conquers the bad guys, and rides away into the sunset—is a useful metaphor for the humanistic consultant. Many successful consultants are loners, counter-dependent to power and structure. Although they professionally help groups and systems function better, a surprising number have low needs for affiliation. When the system they have helped change begins to reap the rewards of increased openness, trust, and collaboration, the practitioner is riding away, unable to participate in the joy she has helped create.

- There are times when the opposite happens. Just as the gunfighter who cleans up the town and becomes, himself, a worse problem than those he's ejected, practitioners have been known to stay too long and serve their own needs rather than the clients. If you are seeking to retain a practitioner do your due diligence and check him out thoroughly before signing him up. Ethical practitioners will push to be very clear about a mutually agreed exit strategy. Talented ones are in demand and won't need to overstay their welcome to simply generate revenue.

- Reflective practitioners are constantly conflicted over the choices they must make over what types of clients they will work with, their tolerance for clients who only allow them to nibble around the edges of true change, the dire needs of potential clients without the resources to hire them, and the societal implications of their client's products. If, as a practitioner, you're concerned over these worries, take heart. If you didn't have them you wouldn't be engaged in the humanistic form of consulting. The best advice is to do unto yourself what you advise your clients to do. Find some-one—probably another consultant—to talk to. Take the time and give yourself the space to externalize your feelings and emotions. If, in the final analysis, the pain of working with a client isn't worth either your anxiety or the potential gain for that client, walk away. Life is too short to waste time on a client who is toxic to your values.

17. Breaking Organizational Codependency

> "Who you are should not be where you work."
> —*Humanistic Consultant*

As a result of downsizings, mergers, global outsourcing, and the "lean and mean" impact of reengineering, there is a widespread, lingering epidemic of job insecurity across most organizational sectors. It affects middle-aged middle managers who are uncomfortable with technology and lack transferable skills. It affects upper level managers who have carved out life styles that are dependent on salaries and bonuses that have evolved more through their tenure than their performance and are significantly out of tune with—assuming they could even find other jobs—what other organizations would be willing to pay. Despite the largely anecdotal reports that millennials and younger employees are "different," they, too, want to hold on to their jobs to pay off their student debts, establish career foundations, and prove their economic independence.

When job insecurity deepens and employee self-esteem becomes contingent on employment continuity; when employees ground their social, emotional, and recreational lives in organizationally defined events and contexts; they are organizationally codependent. Breaking the cycle of organizational codependence is directly compatible with humanistic values and affords the practitioner the opportunity to help unleash repressed creativity, spontaneity, and work-joy.

Traditional Codependency Defined

Initially codependency was used to describe the relationship of a significant other with an alcoholic. Those who denied their feelings, altered their identities, and invested a great amount of energy in the attempt to control an alcoholic, shared the alcoholic's addiction; they were codependent with the alcoholic (Beattie 1987). The idea has now been expanded to cover many other forms of addiction, and codependency is considered by some social scientists to be an underlying, primary disease in itself (Schaef 1986).

A story will illustrate the way a codependent relationship holds the humanistic principles of self-esteem, personal boundaries, and individual responsibility, hostage.

> A woman was mid-way through a long run when the sky darkened and a unexpected thunderstorm erupted. She turned and raced back toward her home but a sudden bolt of lightning hit her. She was knocked unconscious and her heart stopped beating. Luckily she was felled next to a hospital and a team of paramedics rushed to her aid. For a couple of minutes it was touch and go, but they skillfully plied their trade and brought her around. One young medic could not contain his curiosity asked her, "We almost lost you. What did you think about when you were on the brink?"
>
> She wiped the rain from her face, cleared her eyes, looked at him and responded, "As I was dying, my husband's whole life flashed before my eyes."

Organizational Codependence Defined

Just as a person can exist in a codependent state with another person, an employee can be codependent with an organizational system. People who are organizationally codependent have enabled the system to control their sense of worth. They have lost their autonomy and their self-esteem is held hostage to employment continuity. A primary symptom of traditional codependency is that the codependent's sense of value and identity is based on pleasing, and controlling someone else. Organizational codependents take on the impossible task of both trying to control and please the organization so as to prevent job loss. They surrender their self-esteem to organizationally imposed values and organizationally imposed identity.

WHO YOU ARE SHOULD NOT BE WHERE YOU WORK

I first heard this statement from an experienced practitioner and have found it very useful in communicating both the fundamental cause of organizational codependency and the path for breaking its grip. If who you are is where you work, there is a lot more at stake than a paycheck when you are threatened by job loss. It's not just your job that's vulnerable; it's your identity, sense of relevance, and purpose.

ROOT CAUSE

The fundamental cause of organizational codependence is a deep, often not externalized, sense of violation. The psychological contract between employee and organizations has been unilaterally changed and the employee is plagued by feelings of fear, insecurity, and uncertainty. These feelings trigger frustration, resentment, anger and, often, depression. The practitioner, whether in an individual coaching relationship or in group process consultation, needs to find ways to help with symptom relief before engaging in any form of developmental activity. The symptoms don't go away on their own and without assistance often appear to intensify over time.

The Unintended Consequences of "Tying in" Employees

The widespread organizational strategy of finding ways to tie employees in for the long term that evolved during times of stability and predictability has very bad unintended consequences in today's new reality. Employees were seduced into a codependent relationship with their employers. Organizations provided trinkets—key chains, bracelets, watches—that employees wore with pride to publicly celebrate their tenure. Benefits, services, office size, and parking spaces all rewarded longevity. Recreational activities, group travel discounts, and employee clubs and associations served to channel employees' social patterns into organizationally sanctioned outlets. Friendships evolved from the "tie in" strategy and many employees counted most of their friends from within their corporate ranks. Many organizations allowed spouses and close relatives to work in close proximity and the lines between personal and organizational family were blurred.

THE HAZARD OF PUTTING SOCIAL AND EMOTIONAL EGGS IN THE ORGANIZATIONAL BASKET

Organizations reaped what they had sown. The predictable result of the tie in strategy was that many employees put all of their social and emotional eggs in the organizational basket. Who they were was truly where they worked. When the new reality—sometimes called the new psychological employment contract—dawned with accompanying downsizings and reengineering, the basket was dropped, many eggs were broken and those employees who remained were set up for organizational codependency. One reflective senior manager I worked with put it this way, "We tied them in so well that when we downsized, those who we kept were terrified and, to be honest, I'm kind of feeling that way too." The unintended consequences of tying employees in for the "long haul" was that when the predictable long haul gave way to the unpredictable short haul, many employees who remained were plagued by the classic survivor symptoms of guilt, fear and anxiety. They became organizationally codependent.

Unhealthy and Unproductive Coping Mechanisms

At the organizational level, codependent employees are risk-averse and suffer from impaired productivity. Taking risks makes them vulnerable to failure and failure could lead to negative evaluation and potential job loss. They are so self-absorbed with their codependent symptoms, they are unable to form authentic relationships with team members and are not capable of connecting their spirit and energy to their work, resulting in a decline of productivity.

At the personal level employees exhibit the classic codependent behaviors of attempting to control, manipulate, and please the "other" (in the organizational variety, the other is the organization itself), and index their self-esteem and identity on the other's behavior. They scheme and desperately struggle to minimize the threat of separation and their self-image and job satisfaction are held hostage to their success.

The result is a loss for both the employee and the organization. The loss for the organization is that at the very time they need employee creativity and risk-taking to regain momentum, they are fielding a codependent work force that represses creativity and fears taking risks. The loss for the employee is that he becomes more isolated and self-absorbed, increasing his susceptibility to job loss—the exact outcome his codependent behavior seeks to minimize.

Interventions Help Break Organizational Codependency

Breaking the chains of organizational codependency is much easier said than done. In the final analysis, the codependent employee must muster up the courage and insight to free himself. Regardless of talent level or intervention strength, the practitioner can't do it for him. There are some things practitioners can do to stimulate the process.

FACILITATE EMOTIONAL RELEASE

Helping codependents deal with their feelings of violation is critical to the catharsis necessary for letting go and moving forward. A surprising number of organizations have norms against employees even admitting the presence of emotions such as fear and violation, let alone allowing them to share and deal with them in the work place. In these cases, I have engaged in a form of bait and switch. With proper facilitation, group sessions labeled as "team building" or "organizational problem solving" can evolve into productive venting sessions that externalize and, through sharing, validate the ubiquity of debilitating, codependency-stimulated emotional blockages. Based on the positive results of these sessions, this is a case where the intervention end justifies the labeling means.

Individual coaching is a much more straightforward intervention. A skilled humanistic coach can, rather quickly, uncover and work with the client's true needs and organizationally suppressed agenda. Unfortunately, coaching in most organizations is a prerequisite reserved for upper managers and top executives so, regardless of need, those in lower levels are bypassed. Training human resource professionals and operating managers to facilitate productive venting and necessary grieving is a promising option, but one that is not commonly used.

Regardless of how it is done, or by whom—assuming they are fully qualified—helping employees externalize their emotions is a necessary first step toward breaking organizational codependence. It won't automatically solve the problem, but it will make breaking the bonds much easier.

DEVELOP PERSONAL AUTONOMY AND A TASK FOCUS

To break the organizational codependency chain, clients must maintain internal control, keep their personal power, and love themselves without making that love conditional on organizational approval. They must maintain their authenticity, without obsessively and schizophrenically attempting to both please and control the system. The organizational payoff is empowered employees working with minimal control who work because they are invested in the task and interested in a quality product, not because they need to control or please others to maintain their self-esteem. I know of no infallible prescriptive process that will help the client move in this direction. Techniques that have helped in my practice are roleplaying, non-evaluative listening, role-model emulation, scenario forecasting, and, when appropriate, group catharsis.

HELP CLIENTS GROUND SELF-DEFINITION IN "GOOD WORK"

The quest for "good work" is the most important task any of us undertake in our work lives. It means finding work that is a manifestation of our human spirit; work that is in congruence with our individual uniqueness, sense of purpose, and relevance. It doesn't need to be lofty, cerebral, or clean. If serving others is our unique gift, good work can be plain and gritty. Discovering our core purpose and grounding our self-esteem in work that is congruent with that purpose is the key to breaking organizational codependency because we index our self-esteem on our tasks and our work, not the organization where we happen to perform those tasks. Good work always starts internally and is the outward expression of our unique gifts and talents. In its essence, good work is internally goal-driven, not externally relationship-driven. The purpose of good work is to produce something or to accomplish a task of internal value, not to please the boss or impress the system. Pleasing the boss or impressing the system may happen as a consequence of good work, but these consequences are not good work's primary intent. Good work is all about finding work that is nutritious to our human spirit.

Again, I have not discovered any magical formula that will help clients discover the key to good work. Coaching and value clarification that involves opening up and accessing the perspective of trusted others are both very useful, but time consuming, and when either stimulates repressed authenticity, can be an emotionally draining intervention. Discovering work that is nutritious to one's human spirit is a deeply personal journey and the best a practitioner can be is an outside guide.

FACILITATE CLIENT CULTIVATION OF A DIFFUSE ROOT STRATEGY

Breaking organizational codependency begins with a conscious decision not to rely on an employer to nurture all aspects of our lives. The fundamental change that must occur can be most easily illustrated by comparing two types of plants. One plant gets all its nourishment from a single taproot, just as an employee's self-esteem, identity, and social worth can all be nourished by a single organization When we have a social and emotional taproot into an organization we will manipulate, cajole, control, and scheme simply to hang on. Considering the option, manipulating and controlling make sense. What happens if that single taproot gets cut?

Another plant variety has a diffuse root system, reaching out to different areas of soil. Emotionally healthy individuals reject the simplicity and seductiveness of having all their needs nourished through a taproot into the organizational soil. Through planning and effort they can develop a diffuse root system. They can have a number of roots: into their community, professional associations, families, clubs, religions, and friends from outside their places of employment. If the organizational root is cut, they can still function, grow, and thrive.

I have found encouraging clients to diagram their root system a very helpful exercise. It's even more helpful if done in conjunction with a significant other. Many who have tried this are surprised at the extent of their taproot into the organizational system. This discovery can serve as a wake-up call and stimulate them to develop a much broader diffuse root system. I have developed a Susceptibility to Organizational Codependence Index (Appendix A) that has proven useful for clients assessing the adequacy of their root system.

As with diagramming a social root system, completion of the Susceptibility to Organizational Codependence Index has much more value when done by the employee and others who have visibility as to her organizational behavior and values. I have experienced positive outcomes when several people complete the index and compare the results in a group setting. This type of a session is best facilitated by an external practitioner.

The Fallacy of Attempting to Control the Uncontrollable

I often see employees of all levels and generations desperately trying to retain control of decaying and non-productive employment cultures. The old psychological employment contract is dead and holding on to it is energy depleting and non-productive. Younger employees who grew

152

up expecting immediate gratification within a parental and educational bubble that protected them from experiencing failure react to the constraints of the new reality by seeking someone to blame and seldom look within themselves. Managers cling to fantasies of organizational permanence and long-term decision-making. During crises such as mergers and downsizing, controls are intensified, information is managed, the truth is feared and straight talk is driven underground by control talk. Far too many employees interact with their organizations paralyzed by the unarticulated, underlying sense of violation that leads to organizational codependence.

Through coaching, dialogue, roleplays, reality assessment projects, group processes and other interventions, practitioners can be of great assistance to employees at all levels. However, not all interventions are successful and the codependent's need for control is strong. The sad reality is that, no matter how much they try to control the system, codependents are ultimately controlled by it.

The Humanistic Challenge

Organizational codependency is a volatile mix of perceptions and beliefs that violate the humanistic values of employee empowerment, free choice, and autonomy. There is a tremendous upside for both the employee and the organization when codependency is broken. Relationships that are free of unhealthy control and dependency are fun, spontaneous, and creative. Organizations that are free of codependent employees are, similarly, vibrant, open, and productive. They are staffed by employees who are invested in performing good work and led by liberated managers who see their role as helping, not controlling.

No organization is immune to profit swings, downsizing, and mergers, but non-codependent employees are largely immune to survivor sickness. They don't connect their self-esteem and sense of personal worth to the organization, but rather to their own good work. Codependency is dealt a double blow: employees are not unhealthily dependent, and organizations tend to be much more productive and competitive because employees' immunity frees up energy and creativity.

Breaking organizational codependency is a very difficult experience for most clients and a surprising number of internal organization development practitioners. It requires the fortitude to let go of an organizationally imposed identity and venture into the unchartered waters of personal autonomy and relevance. Practitioners can help, but in the final analysis, it requires individual acts of courage. The gain is well worth the pain. Finding work that is in congruence with our unique gifts and grounding our self-esteem and purpose in work that is nutritious to our human spirit is a magnificent quest that will not only help us, but will also help our organizations and our society.

Advice and Recommendations

- Organizational codependence is a widespread and under-diagnosed barrier to employee creativity and organizational productivity. Helping employees free themselves from its stultifying chains is an opportunity for the practitioner to facilitate healthy humanistic values for both the individual and the organization. It is not an easy process. It requires patience, time, and coaching skills.

- If you are an internal consultant, an employee, or a line manager, there is a possibility that you may be a victim of organizational codependency. Review the symptoms outlined in this chapter and assess the degree to which you have an unhealthy taproot into your organization by taking the Susceptibility to Organizational Codependence Index (Appendix A). Have others, including your significant other, complete it and compare the results. If you suspect you're in a codependent relationship get some help. Don't wait, your symptoms will only get worse. It may not be easy to find a competent helper but be persistent. The concept of organizational codependence is not that well known and many organizations have unwritten norms against owning up to or discussing its symptoms.

- Through dialogue, group facilitation, and reality-based coaching, practitioners can help, but breaking organizational codependence ultimately demands individual acts of bravery. It requires the will to disconnect self-esteem from organizational affiliation.

- Organizational codependency is seductive. It is the outcome of nearly a century of organizational strategies designed to tie employees in for the long term. Helping employees cease putting all of their social and emotional eggs in the organizational basket and working with them to promote defining themselves by their work, not where they currently happen to perform that work is difficult but very gratifying when successful.

- If you are a student or an academic researcher, organizational codependence is an under-researched topic that is in need of disciplined study and information dissemination.

18. Nurturing Learning Cultures

"Teams, not individuals, are the fundamental
learning unit in modern organizations."—*Peter Senge*

The Fifth Discipline, Peter Senge's seminal book on organizational learning, came out in 1990—the zenith of the shift to the new reality and the peak of the epidemic of corporate downsizings. It became a best seller because it was informative and organizational leaders were looking for ways to weather the productivity crisis and thrive in the new era. The book stimulated many articles in the popular and academic presses concerning the creation, value, and maintenance of learning organizations.

The development of a learning culture remains a primary objective for many firms nearly 30 years after the publication of *The Fifth Discipline* and is a fertile field for organization development practitioners. Unfortunately, aside from Senge's follow-up *Fieldbook* (1994), much of the published material is either clouded in academic jargon or oversimplified to the level of trivial slogans and labels. This chapter offers practical perspectives for both the manager and the practitioner on the creation of an organizational culture that can facilitate organizational learning.

Practical Perspectives on the Creation of a Learning Culture

ORGANIZATIONAL LEARNING CAN'T BE EXTERNALLY ENGINEERED: OUTSIDE-IN WON'T WORK

Technically organizations can't learn anything, they are shared abstractions and don't exist in a biological sense. To conclude they are capable of learning is to practice reification: the application of human traits to the non-human. This means that you can't do anything *to* an organization and *make* it a learning organization. Top management or outside practitioners can't write a vision statement, hold a workshop, or require a book be read, and decree their organization a learning organization. Organizational learning can't be externally designed and imported. Organizations that have tried this approach ended up with the same people, performing in the same dysfunctional, parochial, and political manner as in the past.

LEARNING CULTURES CAN BE CREATED: INSIDE-OUT DOES WORK

What people can collaboratively do is create organizational cultures that stimulate learning. The phrase *learning culture* is much more useful than *learning organization*. Learning cultures are not engineered, they are behaved. Cultures are formed by people doing things, interacting with each other and establishing norms. As Ross, Smith, Roberts, and Kleiner (1994 48) succinctly put it: "At its essence, every organization is a product of how its members think and interact." The way people create learning organizations is to interact with each other in ways that create a culture that stimulates and reinforces learning. The way practitioners help is to facilitate this interaction. This is an inside-out approach and the only one that works.

BELIEF IN COLLECTIVE WISDOM REQUIRES COURAGE

Behaving in a manner that stimulates organizational learning is a counter-cultural process for many top managers. The most difficult aspect involves refraining from individual decision making, seeking the input of the collective organization, and trusting group decisions. Senge (1990 10) says it this way: "Team learning is vital because teams, not individuals, are the fundamental learning unit in modern organizations. This is where 'the rubber meets the road': unless teams can learn, the organization cannot learn." Since top executives are often judged by their ability to make quick decisions, the patience and perspective to seek the collective voice is sometimes negatively reinforced. Top managers must have faith that a group decision is nearly always better in content, process, and ownership, than an individual decision. Competent coaches can be of great assistance in helping top managers gain this perspective.

WIN/LOSS THINKING SABOTAGES
ORGANIZATIONAL LEARNING

Despite public political correctness and an ecumenical veneer, many top managers have been conditioned to win/loss thinking. Part of this is a carryover from the marketplace where they are rewarded for winning and beating the competition. This "I win, you lose" binary perspective does not work inside organizations. It is anathema to the nurturing of learning cultures. It materializes in mergers why "my" side is better than "your" side and results in dysfunctional infighting. It is found in strategy formulation where "my" way is better than "your" way and leads to wounded egos and missed opportunities. It appears in information analysis where "my" data is right and "yours" is inaccurate. In many top management cultures the norm is argument, debate, and winning when what is really needed is dialogue and learning.

Dialogue is much different than debate or even discussion. Senge (1990 10) differentiates: "Dialogue differs from the more common 'discussion' which has its roots with 'percussion' and 'concussion' literally a heaving of ideas back and forth in a winner-takes-all competition." In order to behave in a manner that stimulates the creation of a learning culture, managers need to stop debating and seeking I win/you lose outcomes. There are corporate "war stories" of executives winning the argument, and losing market share and sometimes their jobs.

Practitioners have two opportunities to be of help. The first involves coaching and helping clients learn how to turn debates into dialogues. Using feedback and roleplaying, I have found most to be willing students. Once they discover that participative dialogue produces better results than win/lose posturing, they are motivated. It is not a rapid transition and requires patience and persistence for both the client and the coach, but, even a small improvement results in disproportionate positive gains.

The second area where practitioners can add significant value is in using their process consultation skills to help surface and repair dysfunctional group behavior. Senge (1990 10) writes:"The discipline of dialogue also involves learning how to recognize the patterns of interaction in teams that undermine learning. The patterns of defensiveness are often deeply engrained in how a team operates. If unrecognized, they undermine team learning. If recognized and surfaced creatively, they can actually accelerate learning."

KILLING MESSENGERS KILLS LEARNING:
HONOR DIVERSE PERSPECTIVES

Killing, or at least wounding, the messenger is a common impediment to the nurturing of a learning culture. People bringing bad news or telling their conception of *truth* are often labeled as whiners, naysayers, whistle-blowers, and pessimists. Organizations with credit-granting roles are sometimes called "sales prevention departments." Staff functions are negatively typecast as "types," as in "green-eyeshade, accounting *types*," "petty obstructionist legal *types*," and goody-goody "human resource *types*." Labeling, stereotyping and discounting peoples' organizational and professional roles serves to disempower them and shut them down. Learning cultures value and honor all data, good and bad. Top managers need to remain open to all messages.

It is always more fun to celebrate good news and easy to like and favor those who bring it. Top managers have to find a way to encourage receiving bad news and views that differ from theirs. If they don't, people will tell them only what they want to hear and they will be deaf to the kind of vital information that will help their organizations and their own judgment improve. Coaches can play a valuable role by helping senior managers reduce their defensiveness and learn how to encourage and accept bad news and contradictory opinions.

Nurturing Learning Cultures in Uncertain Times

In today's volatile global economy, organizations are often attempting to develop and maintain learning cultures against a backdrop of rapid change, increased competition, and economic uncertainty. A long-term client who broke down during a coaching session provides an example.

FACILITATE THE QUEST
FOR PURPOSE AND RELEVANCE

The tears and emotional anguish were in polar opposition to the conservative culture of his firm and his past rational, controlled, behavioral pattern. We had previously worked on issues such as his interactions with his board, relationships with his subordinate vice presidents, and a post-merger strategy. He prided himself on creating a learning culture. Now, as a result of the loss of a large federal contract and global competition, his business was facing massive layoffs, his personal wealth, indexed by the firm's stock price, had significantly eroded, the viability of his firm was uncertain, and his past leadership was being openly questioned. The context of our coaching relationship had precipitously changed to the singular purpose of dealing with his sense of relevance, purpose, and societal contribution. We made limited progress and he was eventually referred to a licensed clinician.

This wasn't an isolated incident. With Middle East unrest, a sustained drop in oil prices, and a slowing of the world economy, I'm finding that nurturing organizational learning is taking place against a backdrop of individual and organizational anxiety. Here are two guidelines to help humanistic practitioners nurture organizational learning in troubled times.

Don't use your definition of help, operate from the definition of the helpee. "Help is defined by the helpee not the helper." As mentioned in a previous chapter, I learned this deceptively simple phrase from the late Pat Williams, founder of the Pepperdine MSOD program. Over the years, I have come to appreciate its profound relevance to a coaching relationship. When a client is caught up in a crisis of purpose, competence, and self-esteem, facts, figures, reports tracking progress against organizational learning objectives, models, 360-degree feedback reports, and flow charts don't help. They only get in the way. Feelings and emotions, not facts and figures, are important. Logical analysis and rational planning may help the coach feel competent, but they will only make the coachee feel worse.

Anyone who has had an argument with a significant other and attempted to defuse that person's emotional issues by logical analysis to prove that they "shouldn't feel that way" will understand that you don't solve a "heart" problem (emotions and feelings) with a "head" (data and logic) process. In a coaching relationship, the more a client's "heart" issues are responded to by the coach's "head" solutions, the wider the empathy gap. Before the client can move forward the basic practitioner behaviors of empathetic listening, reflecting feelings and emotions, and the formation of an authentic, non-judgmental, helping relationship are necessary.

The creation of an organizational learning culture can be facilitated by a subculture that values individual helping relationships. My troubled client confronted his personal issues through an external professional, rebounded, and put his energy into client service and new product development. As a result of his experience, the firm now has an employee assistance program and a structured process of coaching and counseling for all managers and a much stronger learning culture.

Know your limits but be flexible about boundaries. In the case of my troubled client, based on some of the issues he brought up in our coaching sessions, it became clear to both of us that he needed a deeper level of help and he began to work with an external therapist. Our coaching relationship continued and the dual effort resulted in a very positive outcome. As an opposite example, I once managed a bright but inexperienced consultant who lost a valuable client by, when in a very teachable moment, she disengaged and told her client he needed to talk to a licensed therapist. She reacted much too abruptly. Most of his issues were organizational, the result of structural, not personal, issues. We don't have to be licensed clinicians to be good listeners, reflect feelings and emotions, and help our clients articulate debilitating feelings. It is essential to know and adhere to our limits but it is also important that we don't let artificial boundaries limit our abilities to help our clients. Learning cultures have flexible boundaries that bend and sometimes meld when necessary to be effective. Practitioners need to adopt similar approaches to client service.

Advice and Recommendations

- The humanistic practitioner can play a key role in helping organizations build cultures that facilitate learning. A primary requirement is that organizational leaders understand the power of collective wisdom and refrain from past conditioning of making rapid, non-collaborative, individual decisions. Coaching interventions that include behavioral rehearsal and feedback have proven helpful.
- Despite the ubiquitous complaints over too many meetings, organizations are operating in such a complex and rapidly shifting environment that working in groups is a necessity. Most groups are plagued by dysfunctional norms and processes and the practitioner can add great value by helping teams work together more productively and stimulating team learning.
- A fundamental learning technique is the ability to engage in a dialogue, not a debate or a discussion. In a dialogue participants listen to other perspectives, approach the interaction prepared to learn and change their ideas if offered better options, and don't

engage in win/lose games. Dialogue skills have not been the path to most managerial promotions and often need to be explained and taught. Practitioners need to hone their own dialogue skills and then help their clients learn and practice them.

- The ability to form a culture that can learn and adapt is a prerequisite for survival in today's competitive environment. Practitioners can add significant value by helping organizational leaders honor all messages and not punish or devalue bearers of bad news or news that alters preconceived ideas.

- In today's volatile organizational environment, the process of nurturing and sustaining an organizational learning culture, frequently takes place against a background of economic and organizational stress. The practitioner can often be of greatest assistance by temporarily moving out of larger interventions and adopting an individual coaching role.

19. New Reality Management

"Defensiveness and rigidity are counterproductive
in the face of the new organizational reality."
—*Growing, Kraft and Quick*

This chapter is written for the line manager attempting balance a humanistic approach to leadership with the jolting advent of what has been called the new reality. Although there are contextual differences, I use the terms management and leadership interchangeably in this chapter since both are equally affected by the new reality. Organizational leaders are living through a fundamental and irrevocable shift in the way people connect with their organizations and it strikes at the heart of humanistic theory and practice. What has been called the "new paradigm," the "new psychological employment contract," or what can be more plainly be described as the "new reality" at best makes leaders uneasy, and at times, hooks them deeply.

Growing, Kraft, and Quick (1998 xv) articulate the leadership challenge: "A new organizational reality is emerging on the current competitive landscape that is having important, and in some cases adverse, effects on people at work. Defensiveness and rigidly are counterproductive in the face of the new organizational reality." This new reality tests core leadership beliefs concerning such things as loyalty, motivation, and commitment. These beliefs were honed in the old reality and require re-evaluation and change in order to be relevant in the new.

The Old and New Managerial Realities

The old reality or the old paradigm are labels for a pattern of beliefs exemplified by the perception that a person who maintained proper performance and compliance with the organizational culture could count on remaining employed with one organization until voluntary departure or retirement. The reciprocal organizational belief was that loyalty required the individual's total commitment. The organization's response to this commitment and dependence was an acceptance of the obligation to provide a lifetime career.

In the new reality, there is no long-term job security; all employees are temporary. Organizations have no obligation to plan lifetime careers and employees have no obligation to blindly trust that their organizations will take care of them. Although there is some—more based on anecdotal stories than solid research—feeling that millennials "get it" and the new reality fits their values and conditioning, it has been my experience that all ages and levels, regardless of age, specialization, or length of tenure, are uncomfortable with the new reality.

The new reality dawned in the U.S. thirty years ago but the tug of ingrained organizational cultures is very strong and many organizations continue to struggle. Outside the U.S., particularly in familial organizational cultures such as Japan, and in heavily unionized Western European locations, the struggle is more intense.

It is important for the manager to not collude with the organization's natural cultural defense mechanism to resist and attempt to turn back the clock. The change is irrevocable and relevant leaders must find ways to help themselves and their employees deal with it and not waste energy and time fruitlessly developing programs attempting to getting things back to "normal." What has occurred is a fundamental redefinition of the connection between employee and employer. Efforts to tell employees "if you just make these cuts" or "just get with the new program" (quality, reengineering, customer alignment) we will finally get through it and things will return to the way they were, communicate the wrong thing and create false expectations. The nature of the change is that despite the most well-intentioned, well-designed, and badly needed improvement programs, things will never return to the way they were. This is a tough message, but one the humanistic manager must find the courage to deliver.

FOUR COUNTER CULTURAL IMPLICATIONS FOR THE HUMANISTIC ORGANIZATIONAL LEADER

Redefinition of loyalty, motivation, and commitment. Motivation and commitment are not irrevocably bound to lifetime employment, organizational loyalty, and fitting in. In order to be relevant to the true needs of new reality organizations, the manager must find ways to reinforce this shift. Doing it in a command-and-control style won't work; the reaction will be rigidity and defensiveness. The humanistic process of valid data (telling the truth and having the patience and perspective to not get hooked by argument and resistance), free choice (allowing employees to come to their own conclusions and avoiding "I'm right/you're wrong" arguments), and internal commitment (helping employees commit to their work, not permanently to the current organization where they perform that work) is the task of the relevant manager.

Decoupling employee identity from their place of work. It is possible—most likely essential for individual and organizational survival—for people to do excellent work in the service of others without a guarantee of lifetime employment or placing all of one's social, emotional, or financial eggs in the organizational basket. This is a dual task for the manager. First, she must unhook her own identity and sense of contribution from her organizational affiliation, then she needs to help her employees do the same. Decoupling is often much harder for managers and leaders because of their past "old reality" psychological investment in remaining unwaveringly committed to their organization as a part of their leadership role.

Shift in the focus of loyalty. The new reality manager must promote an awareness and acceptance that organizational commitment and productivity are not diminished by loyalty to self, work-team, or profession. Although many organizations have strong cultural norms against articulating the new reality necessary for a shift in loyalty, leaders must find a way to tell the truth.

One way I have seen this accomplished is through partnering with an organization development practitioner in open communication meetings with small groups. If the cultural barriers are too strong for the humanistic manager to pass on the message, the OD practitioner can initiate the necessary truth-telling dialogue.

Redefinition of the management process. The relevant manager in the new reality will be more closely aligned with humanistic values and approaches. The management process is very different in a workforce unencumbered by fear, false expectations of promotions, the distractions of organizational politics, or attempting to impress the boss. The liberated new reality manager will find meaning in helping and facilitating, not controlling or directing.

The Organizational Preference Questionnaire

A useful way to assess comfort with the seemingly harsh and temporary nature of the new reality is the completion of the Organizational Preference Questionnaire, Appendix B. It can be used at the individual, small group, or total systems level. It is a very effective method of stimulating a dialogue among organizational stakeholders and that dialogue will not always initially be positive.

Even though we are well into the third generation of the new reality, there is a significant cultural lag—particularly among top managers—in accepting its implications. In one session with senior executives, the CEO crumpled up his questionnaire, threw it at the humanistic manager who convened the meeting, and walked out of the room. While this CEO's reaction was unusual, less demonstrative resistance is not. Resistance and debate is a testimony to the value of the questionnaire in opening up often-repressed dialogue concerning the irrevocable consequences of the advent of the new reality.

A Prescription for Relevant Leadership

REJECT OUTDATED "COMMANDMENTS"

Our practice and theory are grounded in our experiential and academic "commandments." A commandment is what we have distilled from our cultural conditioning and accept as being "right." For many organizational leaders these commandments were forged in the prosperous business friendly years following World War II. They were built on several implicit assumptions that were shared by employer and employee: the employment relationship should be long term, and organizations should develop strategies and processes to tie employees in over a career; the reward for good performance was promotion; there were predictable and long-term career paths; employees should trust that organizations would take care of them; employers had a mandate to be paternalistic; and that loyal employees did not look for jobs outside the organization. These assumptions are not valid in the new reality.

We are well into the paradigm shift in regard to the relationship of people to organizations. Like it or not, we are all temporary employees. Even with the return to profitability, organizations cannot afford to make a commitment to take care of an employee over a forty-year career, and it is a bad bargain for individuals to put all their social and psychological eggs into one organizational basket. The humanistic manager can make a profound difference by helping both individuals and organizations work through this basic shift in the nature of the psychological employment contract.

Managers must first evaluate their own approach and discard dependence on old reality solutions to new reality issues. Most managers are painfully aware at both a personal and organizational level of the dictates of the new reality but I have witnessed too many with an inability to translate this awareness into relevant action. They become angry and frustrated because they use an ineffective strategy of responding to the stress of the new paradigm by working harder on solutions and perspectives that are artifacts of old reality commandments. It is important that these managers gain a perspective on their intervention and leadership approaches by testing their assumptions and approaches with trusted colleagues or outsiders such as organization development practitioners.

VIEW EMPLOYEES AS SHORT-TERM ASSETS, NOT LONG-TERM COSTS

As an enduring legacy of the new reality, many organizations continue to view employees as costs to be managed and reduced through outsourcing, automation, or downsizing. When employees see themselves only as disposable costs they become defensive and their motivation and self-esteem decline along with customer service and work quality. Relevant managers must find ways to help employees conceptualize their identity as assets to be nurtured and developed—not for a lifetime career—but in the "here and now" of their work. This requires direct, hands-on communication and coaching that celebrates the power of freedom from an organizationally derived identity and the personal affirmation of quality work, autonomy, and customer focus.

Managers are employees too, and not immune to the effects of the new reality on their own motivation and commitment. If you are a manager, remember the adage, "Physician, heal thyself." You can't help your employees if, when you look in the mirror, you see a dollar sign emblazoned on your forehead. You can't communicate the joy of a non-codependent relationship with your organization when you are paralyzed with fear for your own job. Find help. Externalize your feelings. Find someone you trust and talk it through.

VALIDATE NORMATIVE ASSUMPTIONS

The assumptions managers made in the old reality—that employees were motivated by fitting in, pleasing the boss, and doing things "the company way"—do not carry over to the new reality. New reality management is more about facilitating and coaching than controlling and directing. There is no foolproof instruction manual for effective leadership in the new reality. There are too many variables. The external environment has been characterized by the label "RUPT"—Rapid, Unpredictable, Paradoxical, and Tangled. The leadership process can be similarly labeled. Yesterday's leadership approaches will not solve today's problems. New reality leaders need the courage and spirit of experimentation necessary to discard old tools and strategies and seek new, often unproved and intuitive solutions.

BE A MISSIONARY OF HOPE

Despite the emotional barriers to letting go of outdated commandments, there is a very positive upside to the new reality. When employees break organizational co-dependency by putting their self-esteem into what they do, not necessarily where they work, there is a powerful freeing of energy and spirit. This is reflected, paradoxically, in increased job security and organizational productivity. This is good news. Managers can be of great value by personally demonstrating, communicating and celebrating this positive aspect of the new reality.

The Necessity of Systems Interventions

Organizations, too, need to detach, let go, and discover their core purposes. Systems interventions are processes, policies, and organizational cultures that accommodate the new reality. They allow individuals the autonomy to put their spirit into their work, and free organizations to serve customers without becoming paralyzed by internal issues around status and control.

Organizational struggles mirror individual efforts, and it is particularly difficult for many organizations to detach from paternalism. Although some organizations have developed communication themes that emphasize employee autonomy, the provisional nature of the employment contract, and the importance of being "self-employed" within a large organization, these messages are often transmitted in an environment of doubt and confusion. The old paradigm-based assumptions of loyalty, commitment and motivation are deeply entrenched in the operating processes and powerful, often unarticulated, cultural norms of many organizations.

The power of these cultural norms is generally manifested by age and organizational level. Younger, professional employees seem more comfortable with the new reality and are better able to tie their self-esteem to what they do, not where they work. Those in mid-career appear conflicted and confused; while top managers have the most difficult time letting go of the old culture. Because of the confusion and uncertainty, systems interventions—processes and policies that reinforce the new reality—represent a fertile ground for both research and practice.

ESTABLISH SYSTEMS THAT REINFORCE MOVEMENT FROM A LONG-TERM TO A SITUATIONAL EMPLOYMENT RELATIONSHIP

Organizations operating under the old contract had the assumption that employees would be there over the "long haul." They, therefore, developed strategies that rewarded tenure and kept employees tied in over a long-term career. This strategy does not fit the new reality and processes and policies that are more compatible are needed.

Connect the dispensing of symbols, celebrations, and trinkets to strategic intent. Tie bars, cuff links, bracelets, wall plaques, and other public symbols that celebrate tenure give the wrong message when an organization is looking for a flexible, situational employment relationship. As an example, I worked in one organization where the ten-year tenure of a well-liked operational manager was celebrated with a departmental luncheon and the dispensing of bracelet that attested to her ten-year service on a Monday. Her job was eliminated and she was terminated on the following Friday. The employee lost her job. The organization lost credibility.

Achievement, not length of service should be grounds for celebration. Relevant managers find ways to catch people doing things right and find a ways to publicly reinforce positive behavior. There is nothing wrong with trinkets, awards such as dinners or theater tickets, or just pats on the back. It isn't the awards themselves, it is what they are intended to celebrate that is important. The new contract bonds employees and organizations around goal achievement, excellence in customer service and quality work, not around remaining employed. Managers need to develop systems that reward achievement, not tenure.

Departures should be celebrated, not hushed up. Under the new contract, leaving is a cause for celebration not lament. If the goal is a "just in time" work force there will be a continuing flux of arrivals and departures. Leaving is a planned event, a celebration of achievement and past contributions. The departure ritual should be more than just a quiet departmental lunch. It should be an organizationally sanctioned rite of passage.

Remove artificial distinctions between the status and classes of employees. In some organizations today it is difficult to determine from their activities whether a person is a "temp," a "part-time," a "contract," or a "full-time" employee. Artificial distinctions in terms of pay, benefits, and status of these classifications don't fit the new reality. Although there are some legal requirements, themselves artifacts of the old reality, differences, particularly those of status, should be minimized if not eliminated. In the final analysis all employees in the new reality are "temps" and artificial distinctions according to how temporary one is, does not fit the necessary flexibility of the new reality.

MOVE FROM MOTIVATION BY PROMOTION
TO MOTIVATION BY PARTICIPATION

Promotion was the motivational carrot in the old paradigm. What attracts competent employees with transferable skills in the new reality is task investment, job enrichment, the philosophy of quality, and collaborative group efforts such as self-directed work teams.

Engage in job enrichment processes. The concept of job enrichment is a very old idea (Herzberg 1968) that fits new reality leadership. It does not mean, as is the practice with some organizations, adding the duties of departed employees to those who remain. That's job overload, not enrichment. What new reality job enrichment involves is eliminating nonessential tasks and investing employees' energy in relevant, useful, achievable work that is congruent with their unique gifts. If done right, this becomes a positive outcome of the reengineering process (Hammer and Champy, 1993).

The opportunity to perform quality work in an enriched environment replaces promotion as a motivating factor in the new paradigm. It means grounding work in the philosophy of quality as opposed to its often-distracting maze of measurement processes. When separated from its techniques, the philosophy of quality stands for meaningful work performed by empowered people that serves others. This is the liberating upside of the new employment contract.

Install and support self-directed work teams. Semi-autonomous, task focused, self-directed work teams didn't take in the old reality but are a natural fit in the new. Organizations with team-based cultures will have a competitive edge (Shank, 1997). It is, again, necessary to separate technique from essence to gain perspective. The advantage of self-directed work teams is that managers move to a helping, facilitating, and coaching role while empowered teams bond around good work, uninhibited by the hierarchical and bureaucracy constraints of the old reality.

Eliminate Paternalism, Embrace Empowerment

Stop taking care of employees. Most organizations do not like to be labeled as "paternalistic." but a very strong commandment of the old reality was the obligation of organizations to take care of their employees. The unintended consequence was that employees who were *taken care of* became dependent, and, in the new reality, such dependence is hazardous to both their self-esteem and their productivity. An exciting and liberating part of the new reality is the opportunity for all employees to develop the skills and perspectives to take care of themselves, increase their autonomy, and move beyond the constraints of a codependent organizational relationship. Managers can help facilitate employee independence and autonomy by resisting the old reality imperative to take care of employees and not conditioning them into a dependency relationship.

End the myth of long-term career planning. Establishing long-term career paths are an artifact of the old paradigm. Task and skill planning—not career planning—are the stuff of the new reality. In the past, organizations created a dependency relationship by responding to employee requests for maps to get to the top by detailed, often elaborately prepared, professionally illustrated prescriptions as to what tickets needed to be punched. In the new reality, organizations are flat, growth is not hierarchical, systems are temporary, and careers are short-term and situational. Detailed career planning makes no sense when organizations can neither guarantee employment continuity, nor have the ability to forecast the situational and rapidly evolving skills needed over a thirty-year career.

Two basic commandments for the employee in the old reality were: (1) "I need to appear grateful for the privilege of working for this organization," and (2) "I will agree to plan a career within this organization and, if ever dissatisfied, I will never let my manager know that I am looking outside." The reciprocal organizational strategies were: (1) "We will take care of our employees," and (2) "We will promote from within." Two new realities are: (1) In today's volatile global business environment organizations can't keep their end of the bargain, and (2) the organizationally self-defeating result of a rigid internal promotional policy is a narrow and skill-deficient work force. The new reality demands organizational flexibility, employee choice, and non-traditional career paths that often lead outside the organization and sometimes back in again.

There are still some organizations that hold on to the old reality practice of maintaining penalties and barriers for re-hiring employees. They either have policies against re-hiring or penalize those who return through punitive pay and benefit practices. In/out career paths are a central part of the new reality and pay and benefits should not discriminate between those who have remained and those who have returned.

Develop processes that stimulate employee career voice and choice. One model is a mandatory career review at fixed time increments, for example every two years. This review is a time when employees can assess their life and career options in a safe and objective manner and the organization can communicate its assessment of the employee's future options. The result may be a decision to continue in the same job, explore other options within the organization, or leave. Regardless of the mechanics, my experience is that the process is greatly enhanced when facilitated by a third party such as an organization development practitioner or an internal human resource professional.

Tell the truth up front. The unvarnished truth is that organizations can't guarantee employees that, if they do a good job, they can count on continued employment until they either retire or choose to leave on their own. New employees can be offered the opportunity for learning, challenging work, and a safe and clean work environment. Anything beyond that is conjecture. Difficult though it may be for those stuck in old reality commandments, this message should be regularly and consistently communicated, beginning with pre-employment interviews.

The Agony and the Ecstasy of New Reality Interventions

Helping organizations transition into the new reality is neither a gentle nor a spectator sport. Leaders must develop the skills and competencies that will facilitate both their own and their organizations' transition from the certain and comfortable old to the relevant but uncertain and confusing new. Managers must create meaning in a time of profound change. They must stimulate an environment where their reluctant colleagues take the risk of discarding cultural systems that have served their organizations well for nearly a century for those that require a courageous leap of faith. All stakeholders in the system—staff practitioners, managers, and non-managerial employees—must master new or neglected competencies such as transition facilitation, visioning, value congruence, empowerment, self-understanding, and process wisdom.

Organizational leaders need to embark upon a process of continuous self-improvement. No one has yet designed a core curriculum to teach leaders the functional skills necessary to manage a complex business and, in addition, teach them to be authentic, congruent, self-aware, process wise, and other-centered in the midst of major cultural change. Skill development for interventionists is no less challenging. In addition to intervention skills, they need to practice continuous improvement on their intrapersonal insight (self-awareness) and their interpersonal competence (helping and empathy). Relevant humanistic practitioners and operational managers are never done honing their own mind and feelings as the primary instruments of change.

Relevant leadership in the new reality is often a lonely effort that requires tenacity and courage. Changing traditional systems that are grounded in past culturally derived commandments is very difficult for entrenched organizational leaders—particularly those at the top who have worked their way up the ranks over a long-term career—to accept. There is, however, no more important task for the humanistic manager than helping their entrenched colleagues grasp the link between new reality systems and organizational productivity, profitability, and long-term viability.

Advice and Recommendations

- Coming to grips with the altered tenets concerning motivation, loyalty and commitment ushered in by the new reality is a challenge to all types of employees and all levels of management. Helping organizations develop systems and processes that accommodate these changes is the essence of relevant, new reality management.

It is a task that requires courage and commitment but will differentiate those companies that survive from those that sink by refusing to let go of outdated, old reality commandments.

- Completing the Organizational Preference Questionnaire (Appendix B) is a useful way to assess individual and support system new reality accommodation. I have found it an excellent frame of reference to engage clients in grasping the organizational implications of the new reality. When done in a group setting it often results in venting and followed by productive dialogue.

- If you have been with the same firm in a managerial role for a number of years, you may be surprised at the degree to which you have assimilated the commands and culture of the old reality. Before you can be helpful to your organization, you need to work on yourself. I strongly suggest you find a coach who is familiar with the demands of the new reality. An experienced external practitioner would be an excellent choice.

- You probably know in your head that what worked in the past won't transition to the future. However, the pull of past cultural beliefs is more in the heart than in the head. Don't collude with your peer managers that past assumptions concerning loyalty, motivation, and commitment will outlast the new reality. That won't happen. Find a competent helper who can facilitate your natural emotional venting and work to build a bridge to the new paradigm.

- Humanistic managers can play a vital role in the transition from the old to the new organizational reality. They have the opportunity to help organizations form structures and processes that shed the limitations of the old, control-oriented, culture. The payoff for employees is relevance and work that is in congruence with their human spirit. For the organization it is global competitiveness and survival.

20. The Right Stuff

"I knew what they needed but they wouldn't
listen to me."—*Derailed practitioner*

The Right Stuff was a 1983 Academy Award–winning film adaptation of Tom Wolfe's best-selling book that profiled test pilots and the early days of the manned space program. As indicated in Chapter 5, an experienced practitioner responded to a question concerning what she was doing in a large business organization with a terse, "I'm doin' some stuff in one of their divisions." Knowing that practitioner, I am sure she was not just doing stuff but doing "the right stuff." This chapter outlines ten dimensions of the necessary right stuff for humanistic practitioners, and provides background for self-evaluation questionnaires to help uncover any gaps.

Doing the Wrong Stuff: A Case Study

The person that I'll call Jerry had a master's degree in industrial/organizational psychology along with three years' experience in staffing and benefits administration in a corporate human resources role. He attended a seminar on organization development, went to a National OD Network conference and emerged as a passionate convert. He transferred to an OD department in a large operating division of his firm and spent nearly a year learning the ropes by shadowing two experienced practitioners. That division only had a need for two OD professionals and Jerry moved to a one-person practitioner role in a self-contained, medium-sized division. By virtue of education, experience, and interest he should have been a success but nine months into his new job he was fired and, at last report, was working for an outplacement firm. During his exit interview he made a telling statement that precisely articulated the reason for his demise: "*I* knew what they needed but they wouldn't listen to *me*."

Jerry had good academic credentials, the benefit of two excellent

175

mentors, and a conceptual grasp of several intervention strategies. The problem was he got OD in his head but not his heart or his feet. He came across as arrogant, prescriptive, manipulative, and self-serving—not the requisite style for someone whose mission was to help people behave in the opposite manner by becoming more open, non-judgmental, and other-centered. The few times he actually worked with groups, he was rude, directive, and insensitive to personal relationships and group norms. He didn't walk his talk and lost credibility with his clients. He spent the last two months of his OD career isolated in his office, writing long, judgmental, prescriptive emails to the managers he was supposed to help and coach. He never got it that it didn't matter what *he* wanted and what he prescribed, it was what his clients wanted and psychologically *owned* that mattered. It was his job to facilitate that ownership, not order or prescribe it.

William Crockett, an internal OD manager, put his finger on the primary reasons for Jerry's derailment during an interview for the *Journal of Applied Behavioral Science* (Cahn 1978 234). When asked what his expectations for internal practitioners were, he said there were two: "The first is a basic understanding of people and group dynamics so that they can go into groups and help with relationships and process. The second is a modeling of behavior, openness, directness, and confrontation. We expect a person to have credibility with groups in order to influence groups." Crockett's expectations are encompassed in the ten requisite competencies for authentic, right stuff–directed, OD practice.

The Right Stuff: Ten Requisite Competencies for Authentic Practice

OTHER-CENTEREDNESS

Humanistic practice is a helping relationship and the person receiving that help is the client, not the practitioner receiving help in validating her prescription as to the nature of that help. Jerry was self-centered—he knew what the client needed and it was the client's job to understand that need. A powerful adage that practitioners striving for the right stuff should permanently brand into any intervention strategy is that help is defined by the person receiving it, not the person giving it. The authentic practitioner defines her effectiveness through the eyes, spirit, and behavior of the client.

Value Congruence

Richard Byrd (1987) used the term "value congruence skills," to describe the process of behaviorally walking one's talk. Authentic humanistic practice, whether it involves executive coaching, leadership development, or organization development requires living the values one is attempting to impart. The practitioner who is prescriptive, judgmental, and cynical while working to develop an open, facilitative, participative client style will, as was the case with Jerry, rapidly lose credibility. The best practitioners practice what they preach—in a sense they *are* what they preach—they role model humanistic values. Faking it simply doesn't work. Clients see through the act every time.

Developmental Optimism

Authentic practitioners share the enduring value first articulated by Tannenbaum and Davis (1969) that people are not "fixed" but in "process." They view people as assets to be nurtured and developed, not as "things" to be factored into the production equation or costs to be controlled. They have a mission to help people find meaning in their work as a means to instilling purpose in their life. Discovering that purpose is not without struggle. Psychiatrist Victor Frankl credited his survival from Nazi death camps with his ability to hold on to a vision of his life's meaning and purpose. He articulated the fundamental developmental task of the humanistic practitioner when he wrote (1984 127): "We should not, then, be hesitant about challenging man with a potential meaning for him to fill.... What man actually needs is not a tensionless state but rather the striving and struggling for a worthwhile goal."

Practitioners are not in the business of practicing logotherapy, Frankl's version of existential psychiatry, but, if they are attuned to humanistic values, they are involved in helping clients find meaning and purpose in their work. Since clients spend much of their life in the work place, their work is inexorably intertwined with their life's meaning.

Self-Awareness

Practitioners are only human and not without biases, perceptual distortions, social preferences, and emotional needs. The effective ones don't deny their preferences and needs but strive to make them clear and find ways to factor that awareness in to their practice. Jerry had a strong need to control others and be recognized as an expert. When working with other OD consultants during his shadowing apprentice time, he was able to control these needs by assuming supportive roles and adhering to his mentors' behavioral feedback. Once on his own, he lacked both the awareness and the will to self-regulate and focus on a client-centered helping relationship, rather than the satisfaction of his own needs. A central component of emotional intelligence is self-regulation (Goleman 2006) and effective practitioners need to understand their own motivational and perceptual orientations and have the strength to regulate them in the service of their clients. This often requires partnering with another practitioner with offsetting skills and perspectives.

Self-Renewal

It is extremely difficult for the practitioner to exhibit his "A" game over an extended period of time without burning out. Being authentic, congruent, and caring in organizational cultures that often reinforce the opposite behaviors can, as succinctly stated by Bill Norris (Jensen 2013) "grind down" the most resilient practitioner. Too many talented practitioners have become jaded and cynical and end up leaving the field for lack of making the necessary investment in self-renewal. For the external practitioner, self-renewal means stepping back and taking a time out from client interaction. Along with simply taking a time out, connecting with empathetic colleagues, attending conferences, learning new skills or becoming certified in new instruments are useful renewal activities. Any short-term loss of income is a necessary long-term burn out insurance premium and definitely worth the cost.

The task is more difficult for the internal practitioner who must live with her clients. Taking a physical or emotional time out is not part of most corporate cultures. The constant pressure to appear relevant and "earn" their paycheck often makes the need for some form of renewal more acute than that of their external colleagues. Attending conferences, after-hours peer gatherings, and short-term role changes are useful renewal strategies. A very small number of corporations have experimented with sabbatical-like processes and educational leaves but the trend hasn't caught on and has caused internal problems with other disciplines that demand similar treatment. Unfortunately, the burn out of internal practitioners has driven some into a doctor-patient or pair-of-hands role and away from humanistic practices.

Regardless of the organizational barriers for internals and the financial sacrifices for externals, in order to stay relevant, all practitioners need to find ways for periodic self-renewal. As talented and self-aware as most practitioners are, self-diagnosis is a challenge. It is always a good idea to seek the perspective of a trusted colleague.

An Adequate Tool Kit

The saying that if the only tool one has is a hammer, the whole world is a nail, holds true in the universe of humanistic practice. Relevant practitioners have access to a broad array of intervention techniques, diagnostic tools, and assessment instruments. The choice of which one to use and how to apply it depends on the client, the presenting issues, and the mutual client/practitioner diagnosis. A recipe for the wrong stuff involves the practitioner who is wedded to a single or a very limited range of interventions and diagnostic processes.

Understanding the Client's Mission

Based on the work of Dave Ulrich (1997), there is a widespread view among the human resource community that HR should become a "business partner" with operating management. Another common way of phrasing the concept is that HR should find a way to secure "a seat at the management table." While a laudable objective for the human resource professional, for the humanistic consultant, becoming too involved in the management process is at best a distraction and can cross the line into traditional management consultation and result in a loss of the necessary marginality.

Rather than partner in the business or gain a seat at the table, what is really important for the practitioner is insight into the client's mission—his ultimate purpose as a person and his organization's contribution to society. For individuals, it's their sense of personal fulfillment and contribution. For business organizations, it is always something deeper than making money or return on equity. Not that making money isn't essential, but with enough digging the practitioner can discover a deeper purpose: a mission to, in some manner, contribute to society.

The best humanistic practitioners are very adept at discovering their client's personal mission and formulating their helping relationship around this anchor. I once heard an experienced practitioner described as "amazingly able to hook a client deeply." Upon observation, it became clear that this consultant was very skilled at both helping the client discover his personal mission, and engaging with that client in a mutual process of connecting that personal mission with an organizational intervention strategy.

The most effective interventions and the deepest client-practitioner relationships are embedded in the connection between the client's personal mission, the organizational mission, and a mutually planned intervention. All successful humanistic consultants engage in this process. There is no universal formula but it is an essential component of relevant consultation.

GROUP FACILITATION COMPETENCE

Whether the practitioner is involved in organization development, leadership development, or coaching, the odds are significant that she will be working with groups. Today's organizations are far too complex and require too much interactive communication to function without them. The ability to read group dynamics, facilitate balanced participation, and help form norms that build on diversity and maximize productivity is a basic practitioner skill.

Jerry, in the example that began this chapter, lacked this fundamental skill and it was a partial reason for his derailment. Group facilitation skills are to the practitioner what basic literacy is to the high school graduate. The functionally illiterate graduate won't make it in today's world and the would-be practitioner without adequate group facilitation skills will soon join Jerry in another line of work.

CLARITY ON THE INDIVIDUAL AS CLIENT

Organization development received its name in order to emphasize a change in focus from individual to group development. It has been consistently defined as some dimension of planned change and that change is most often defined by the organizational system. The result has too often been a horse-versus-cart issue, with the practitioner overdosing on the cart.

In an ontological sense, organizations don't exist. They are shared abstractions created by people. In order to change the organization (the cart), practitioners need to change the people (the horses), the creators and pullers of the cart. Large systems change, structural interventions, tampering with the reward and punishment systems, and macro process flow analysis are all useful techniques, but if overdone they only redistribute the contents of the cart and ignore the horse.

The most relevant practitioners start with the horse and move to the cart, not the other way around. They ground their interventions in the vision, the mission, and the change options of the individual before attempting to change the system. It is not an either/or process. They seamlessly combine individual and systems change, partnering with their client in mutual horse-and-cart analysis and intervention strategy.

A fundamental question for the confused practitioner seeking help is, "Who is the client?" If the answer is the company, the division, or the department, a large red flag emerges. The client is always a specific person, and not the shared abstraction called an organization.

CONGRUENCE WITH HUMANISTIC PRINCIPLES

The bedrock of humanistic practice is the belief that people have the right and responsibility to give meaning to their lives and organizational creations. Interventions rest on the principles of free choice, inclusion, participation, and societal responsibility. The practitioner or operating manager who relies on coercion, manipulation and hierarchical oppression is not operating in congruence with humanistic principles.

The Consulting Behaviors Inventory

Appendix C, the Consulting Behaviors Inventory, can be used in two ways. The first is as a self-evaluation checklist. There are no right or wrong answers. No practitioner is perfect and the questionnaire is one way to get a reading on self-development goals. Another way to use it is to have people who know the practitioner's work complete it. Again, the purpose is to close developmental gaps and an external review can be a useful reality check on self-ratings.

How to Get the Right Stuff

There is no magic formula and I know of no experienced practitioner who consistently scores ones and twos on the Consulting Behaviors Inventory. Relevant practitioners develop and maintain their skills through a combination of apprenticeship, organizational experience, role model emulation, constructive feedback, reflection, seminars, workshops, formal education, and trial and error. The foundational ingredient is belief and trust in humanistic values. These can't be absorbed in a class or adopted from a mentor. They are the result of early childhood experiences, healthy self-esteem, and cultural conditioning.

An intriguing but impractical and arrogant model is the way Plato visualized the training of philosopher-kings. After passing three successively difficult examinations that would weed out all but a very few, the remainder would be allowed to study philosophy. They would be at least thirty years old and would spend five years in rigorous philosophical training. They would then be turned back to society for fifteen years and be expected to earn a living with no special privileges. At age fifty, they would be ready to assume positions of leadership as philosopher-kings (Durant 1953 31).

Humanistic practitioners are not kings, queens, or philosophers. They are just normal people trying to make a living and make the organizational world a better place. However, Plato's prescription of formal education, real world experience, and natural maturation is a useful conceptualization of the kind experiential grounding that would help them acquire the right stuff.

The Ultimate Right Stuff: Applied Human Spirit

The right stuff is both a means and an end. The means equip the practitioner and the manager with the tools and skills to access and harness the end: the ultimate right stuff—the transformative power of human spirit. Until the advent of the new reality it felt unscientific and culturally sketchy to openly discuss the centrality of human spirit to humanistic practice. It was subsumed in other contexts. It was the "Y" that was contrasted with the control-oriented "X" in Douglas McGregor's (1960) classic theory. It was the "esprit," of the esprit de corps. It was what was sought when we looked for something greater than ourselves in the twelfth step. It was the "joy" in Connelly's (1984) work-joy.

In the old reality, human spirit was undervalued, suppressed, or ignored. It couldn't be precisely measured, manipulated, or contained in an organizational chart. "Spirit" was a word that, among many traditional line managers, conjured up images of cults, psychedelic happenings, and counter-cultural crazies. It was a word that practitioners were reluctant to use in client settings.

WHY HUMAN SPIRIT NEEDS TO COME OUT
OF THE ORGANIZATIONAL CLOSET

The most valuable employees are those who choose to be in an organization. They are much more productive and creative than those who are forced to be there. Pay and benefits are not enough. What will attract this type of employee is meaningful work in the service of others and meaningful work is work that captures the human spirit. When people are working at their best and investing their spirit in their work, they are vastly more productive and creative. Organizations desperately need this applied human spirit as a competitive advantage.

Liberated employees are delightful to manage. When organizations create a culture that nurtures human spirit, management changes from the grim, unrewarding grind of attempting to motivate people whose work does not engage their essence, to the delightful task of coaching liberated employees who are self-motivated and internally directed. Leading the liberated is a much better use of a manager's time than attempting to motivate the dispirited.

The New Glue

In a discussion between two colleagues, one a psychologist schooled in what has sometimes been called "prairie empiricism," and the other a humanistic organization development practitioner, the empiricist postulated that anything that couldn't be measured couldn't be studied. The organization development practitioner spoke of love and beauty before responding that anything that could be reduced to measurement would be too trivial to merit study. The basic ingredient of the new glue that holds successful new reality organizations together—human spirit—would appeal to both.

When people are truly connected to their work through their human spirit, it is reflected through measurement tools such as productivity indexes, attitude surveys, and the most basic of all: sustained improvement to a bottom line. One can also feel it. We have all been in organizations where we can tell that people are "tuned in," and "turned on," but have not as the sixties expression puts it, "dropped out." In fact, they have "dropped in."

Organizations that engage at the level of human spirit do not tolerate sideline sitters. Connecting at this level is not a spectator sport. An outside observer can, indeed, feel it. "It" is a creative, vibrant, and vigorous work place. When humanistic practitioners experience a work environment rich in applied human spirit, they never forget it. It is a tangible target for interventions in other, less "turned on" organizations.

HOW PRACTITIONERS CAN EASE HUMAN SPIRIT OUT OF THE CLOSET

To psychotherapist Carl Rogers the key to establishing a helping relationship is unconditional positive regard: there is a kernel of hope and goodness inside everyone that will grow with enough encouragement and support. The way to kindle human spirit in organizations is to emulate Rogers. Two old reality managerial orientations that get in the way are excessive control and a judgmental attitude. It isn't that organizations don't need some control, or that exercising prudent judgment isn't important. It's that for the new glue to work its magic, leaders need to have a very light hand on the controls. Here are four ways managers and practitioners can partner to promote a climate that cultivates the power of human spirit.

Eliminate those policies, processes, and cultural commandments that are barriers to the development of human spirit. Examples include excess controls, narrow job descriptions, inflexible performance measurement systems, organizational climates which instill risk aversion and fear of failure, rigid barriers to job entry based on artificial standards, and false status distinctions such as those between exempt and non-exempt or managerial and professional job categories.

Stimulate voice and choice. There is great power in the humanistic value of participation and, if organizational leaders are serious about leveraging human spirit as a competitive advantage, very little downside risk. How work gets done, who does the work, performance standards, and processes that allow employee development and training, are all opportunities for employee participation and choice.

Be developmentally optimistic. Organizations can no longer guarantee long-term employment but they can offer employees the opportunity to learn and develop. It goes beyond job-related skills training. If an employee's interest and spirit leads to an area where the rules say she isn't qualified, the wise manager will take a developmental risk. Human spirit has an amazing ability to overcome barriers and developmental optimism is a tangible manifestation of unconditional positive regard.

Engage in continuous nurturing. For the past forty years, management and quality gurus have stressed the importance of *continuous improvement*. In order to reach that goal, something more basic needs to be added to the equation: *continuous nurturing.* Human spirit is a fragile commodity. The key to maintaining it is constant attention to the basics. It is similar to tending a garden; the flowers will grow and blossom only if the gardener pulls the weeds, nourishes the soil, and applies the water. Practitioners of the new reality need to continue to work at eliminating barriers (the equivalent of weeding), fostering participation (nourishing the soil), and maintaining a developmentally optimistic climate (watering the garden).

The Transformative Potential of the Right Stuff

Tom Wolfe's aptly titled book *The Right Stuff* (1979), referenced at the beginning of this chapter, chronicled the pioneering efforts of the test pilots and astronauts in the early stages of the manned space program— an effort with the potential to expand humankind's conception of the universe. Humanistic practitioners and organizational managers can't apply their own right stuff to the exploration of the universe, but they do have the opportunity to shape and develop organizations that are highly productive, open, and have the potential to foster a more inclusive and humane society.

By harnessing the power of applied human spirit to organizations of all types—for profit, non-profit, government, religious, global and local— humanistic leaders and practitioners can truly make this a better world. It is not an easy task, but one that justifies the passion and vision of the pioneers of organization development and transformation and is congruent with the values of humanism.

Advice and Recommendations

- A central component of "right stuff" competencies is an above average degree of emotional intelligence. Humanistic practitioners need proficiency in the five key dimensions of emotional intelligence (Goleman 2006). They need to be *self-aware* (know their own emotions and drives and recognize their impact on others); have the ability to *self-regulate* (control and redirect disruptive emotions); possess relevant *social skills* (be competent at facilitating and influencing relationships); form *empathetic* client relationships (be genuinely able to relate to client emotions); and possess the *motivation* to help others.

- Not walking the talk—behaving in ways that don't demonstrate humanistic values—sabotages credibility. Practitioners are always on stage and clients are always assessing the degree of congruity between their message and their behavior. Faking it won't work, clients can tell the difference. In many ways the practitioner has to *be* her intervention.

- The Consulting Behaviors Inventory in Appendix C is a useful tool, but it is only a tool. If you are a practitioner, don't be too hard on yourself. Very few will rate themselves or receive external ratings of all 1s. However, honest ratings of all 5s and 6s are a reason to seriously consider a career change.

- The foundation of right stuff competencies is belief and faith in the humanistic principles of free will, personal responsibility, human dignity, inclusion, and participation. There is no half way. Without this foundation a person can be exceptionally talented but will not be a humanistic practitioner.

Appendices:
Self Assessments

Appendix A, the Susceptibility to Codependence Index, charts the extent to which an employee's values are grounded in pleasing and controlling his employer. It is useful when completed in isolation, but much more powerful when completed with others and the results compared and discussed in a group setting with the assistance of a skilled external facilitator.

Appendix B, the Organizational Preference Questionnaire, measures comfort with the seemingly harsh reality of the new reality and acceptance of the new psychological employment contract. When the individual results are discussed in a group setting it is a very useful tool in stimulating a dialogue and encouraging productive venting.

Appendix C is the Consulting Behaviors Inventory. It assesses the degree of consulting behavioral congruence with the values and perspectives of humanism. It is useful when completed as an individual and even more beneficial when completed by those who know the consultant and have experienced her work.

Appendix A: Susceptibility to Organizational Codependence Index

1 = Almost all/to a great degree
2 = Most/to a large degree
3 = Some/to an average degree
4 = A few/to a slight degree
5 = Very few/to an insignificant degree

How much of my social life revolves around my business and organizational affiliation?	1 2 3 4 5
How many of my friends are part of my organizational affiliation?	1 2 3 4 5
To what degree are my recreational interests (golf, tennis, travel, etc.) associated with my business or organizational affiliation?	1 2 3 4 5
To what degree is my sense of purpose, relevance and importance associated with my title, level, and organizational affiliation?	1 2 3 4 5
How organizationally specific are my skills and how difficult would it be to transfer them to another organization?	1 2 3 4 5
What would be the impact on my self-esteem if I lost my job tomorrow?	1 2 3 4 5
To what degree are my support systems (people and resources that can help me through difficult times) centered on my organizational affiliation?	1 2 3 4 5
To what degree is my job the center of my life?	1 2 3 4 5
My spouse or significant other thinks I invest too much of my social and emotional life in my job.	1 2 3 4 5
Who and what I am is where I work.	1 2 3 4 5

Total _____

10–25 High Risk
25–35 Moderate Risk
35–50 Low Risk

Pay special attention to items evaluated as 1 and 2

Appendix B:
Organizational Preference
Questionnaire

In this questionnaire you are asked to rate your organization in regard to cultural and systems preferences concerning the psychological employment contract between organization and employee. For each item, choose a number on the continuum that best depicts your perception of your organization's practices. For the most useful results, choose the number that reflects actual practices, not the way you think they should be.

1. **Sharp differentiation between the status of full-time, part-time, and temporary employees; OR little differentiation—difficult to distinguish between them.**
   Clear differentiation   1 2 3 4 5 6   **Little differentiation**

2. **Benefits, services, recognition, and status systems that reward time spent with the organization; OR systems that are tenure free.**
   Tenure-based systems   1 2 3 4 5 6   **Tenure-free systems**

3. **Promotion viewed as primary reward for performance; OR reward and recognition systems tied to factors other than promotion.**
   Promotion-based   1 2 3 4 5 6   **Non-promotion-based**
   systems   **systems**

4. **Support services that "take care" of employees and tie them to the organization; OR systems that provide only the essentials (e.g., health care) and promote employee independence.**
   Take care, tie in   1 2 3 4 5 6   **Essentials only,**
   promote independence

5. **Organization emphasizes long-term detailed career planning: OR focuses on short-term job training.**
   Career planning   1 2 3 4 5 6   **Job training**

6. **Culture of internal growth, external hiring at entry levels only; OR external hiring practiced at all levels.**
   Internal growth   1 2 3 4 5 6   **External hiring**

7. Relationships, proper attire, and fitting in key to success; OR task-specific performance key to success.

    Fitting in   1 2 3 4 5 6   Performing tasks

8. External job searches done in secrecy, employees made to feel disloyal for looking outside; OR external exploration encouraged and organizationally sanctioned.

    Looking outside   1 2 3 4 5 6   Looking outside
    disloyal   encouraged

9. Implicit understanding that employees can count on their jobs with acceptable performance; OR explicit communication that employment is situational and employees can't, even with good performance, count on their jobs for life.

    Long-term assumption   1 2 3 4 5 6   Short-term
                                             communication

10. The primary management tasks are directing, controlling, and analyzing; OR the primary tasks are helping, empowering, and coaching.

    Directing   1 2 3 4 5 6   Helping

11. Job descriptions are important, fixed, and hierarchically linked to the authority structure; OR they are not important, flexible, and separate from the authority structure.

    Important and fixed   1 2 3 4 5 6   Not important and
                                             flexible

12. Organizational leaders do not possess or value transition facilitation skills; OR transition facilitation is a core leadership competency.

    Not valued   1 2 3 4 5 6   A core competency

13. The culture requires planned, controlled, and non-emotional managerial communication about "sensitive" subjects; OR sensitive communication is direct, spontaneous, and expressions of feelings and emotions are encouraged.

    Planned and   1 2 3 4 5 6   Spontaneous and
    controlled   emotional

14. Pay systems are long-term, fixed, and hierarchically arrayed; OR flexible, project-based, and dependent on individual contribution.

    Hierarchically   1 2 3 4 5 6   Task dependent
       dependent

15. Voluntary departures are "uncomfortable," ignored, and communication is suppressed; OR they are celebrated and widely communicated.

    Uncomfortable/   1 2 3 4 5 6   Celebrated/
    ignored   communicated

ORGANIZATIONAL PREFERENCE QUESTIONNAIRE SCORING KEY

15–30: Strong old psychological employment contract orientation.
21–45: Tendency toward old psychological employment contract orientation.
46–59: Middle of the road.
60–75: Tendency toward new psychological employment contract orientation.
76+: Strong new psychological employment contract orientation.

LEADERSHIP SUBSCALE (QUESTIONS 10, 12, AND 13)

3–6: Strong old psychological employment leadership orientation.
7–9: Tendency toward old psychological employment contract leadership orientation.
10–11: Middle of the road.
12–15: Tendency toward new psychological employment contract leadership orientation.
16+: Strong new psychological employment contract leadership orientation.

Appendix C:
Consulting Behaviors
Inventory

In this inventory you are asked to rate your consulting behavior and values. For each item, choose a number on the continuum that best depicts your perception of your consulting behavior. For the most useful results choose the number that reflects the way you actually behave, not the way you think you should behave.

1. *Other-centeredness*: **Focus on the client's self-described needs; OR focus on your prescription of what the client needs**
   Client's description   1 2 3 4 5 6   **Your prescription**

2. *Value congruence*: **Models desired client behavior; OR behaves in opposite manner**
   Models desired   1 2 3 4 5 6   **Behaves in opposite**
   behavior   **manner**

3. *Developmental optimism*: **Helps client find meaning and purpose to their life and work; OR meaning and purpose discovery not part of consultation**
   Helps discover   1 2 3 4 5 6   **Meaning and purpose**
   meaning and purpose   **discovery not part of**
                                             consultation

4. *Self-awareness*: **Aware and able to self-regulate personal needs and biases; OR unaware and unable to self-regulate**
   Aware and able to   1 2 3 4 5 6   **Unaware and unable**
   self-regulate   **to self-regulate**

5. *Self-renewal:* **Invests time and energy in self-renewal; OR doesn't engage in self-renewal activities**
   Invests in self-renewal   1 2 3 4 5 6   **Doesn't engage in**
                                                    self-renewal

6. *An adequate tool kit:* Able to access a broad range of diagnostic and intervention tools; OR has a limited range of tools
   Broad range   1 2 3 4 5 6   Limited range

7. *Understands client mission:* Works to discover personal and organizational mission; OR discovery of mission not part of consultation
   Understands client and   1 2 3 4 5 6   Discovering missions
   organizational mission   not part of consultation

8. *Group facilitation competence:* Has group facilitation skills; OR group facilitation not a core skill
   Competent group   1 2 3 4 5 6   Group facilitation not
   facilitator   a core skill

9. *Clarity of individual as client:* Is clear on importance and identity of individual client; OR unclear and sees system as client.
   Clear on individual   1 2 3 4 5 6   Unclear, sees system
   as client   as client

10. *Congruence with humanistic principles:* Is guided by humanistic values; OR doesn't behave in accordance with values
    Guided by   1 2 3 4 5 6   Not guided by
    humanistic values   humanistic values

CONSULTING BEHAVIOR INVENTORY SCORING KEY

10–20: Strong orientation toward humanistic practice.
21–49: Middle of the road.
50–60: Strong orientation away from humanistic practice.

References

Ackerman Anderson, L. 2016. Organization Development and Transformation. In Rothwell, W., Stavros, J., and Sullivan R. (Eds.) *Practicing Organization Development: Leading Transformation and Change*, 60–77. New York: Wiley.

Ackerman Anderson, L., and Anderson, D. 2010. *The Change Leader's Roadmap: How to Navigate Your Organization's Transformation*, 2nd ed. San Francisco: Pfeiffer

Adams, J. (ed.) 1984. *Transforming Work*. Alexandria, VA: Miles River Press.

_____. (ed.) 1998. *Transforming Work*, 2nd ed. Alexandria, VA: Miles River Press.

Allen R., and Kraft, C. 1984. Transformations That Last: A Cultural Approach. In Adams, J. (ed.) *Transforming Work*, 36–54. Alexandria, VA: Miles River Press.

Appelbaum, S. 1993. *A Psychologist Explores Alternate Therapies: Out in Inner Space*. Northvale, NJ: Jason Aronson.

Arlow, J. 1979. Psychoanalysis. In Corsini R. (ed.) *Current Psychotherapies*, 2nd ed. 1–43. Itasca, IL: F. E, Peacock.

Argyris, C. 1970. *Intervention Theory and Method: A Behavioral Science View*. Reading, MA: Addison-Wesley.

Arnold M. 1867. Dover Beach. In Ward, C. (ed.) *Dover Beach and Other Poems*, 86. Mineola, NY: Dover publications Inc.

Athos, G., and Gabarro, J. 1978. *Interpersonal Behavior: Communication and Understanding in Relationships*. Englewood Cliffs, NJ: Prentice-Hall.

Bass, B., and Avolo, B. (Eds.), 1994. *Improving Organizational Effectiveness Through Transformational Leadership*. Thousand Oaks, CA: Sage.

Beattie, M. 1987. *Codependent No More: How to Stop Controlling Others and Start Caring for Yourself*. San Francisco: HarperOne.

Bellman, G. 2002. *The Consultant's Calling: How to Bring Who You Are to What You Do*. San Francisco: Jossey-Bass.

Bennis, W., Benne, K., and Chin R. (Eds.), 1961. *The Planning of Change*. New York: Holt Rinehart and Winston.

Berne, E. 1964. *Games People Play*. New York: Grove Press.

Bion, W. 1961. *Experiences in Groups*. New York: Basic Books.

Block, P. 2000. *Flawless Consulting*, 2nd ed. San Francisco: Jossey-Bass/Pfeiffer.

Bradford, L. 1974. *National Training Labs: Its History: 1947–1970*. Bethel, ME: National Training Labs.

Brownell, P. Gestalt Therapy: *A Guide to Contemporary Practice*. New York: Springer Publishing Company.

Buckingham, W., Burnham, D., Hill, C., King, P., Marenbon, J., and Weeks, M. 2011: *The Philosophy Book: Big Ideas Simply Explained*. New York: DK Publishing.

Burns, J. 1978. *Leadership*. New York: Harper & Row.

Byrd, R. 1987. Corporate Leadership Skills: A New Synthesis. *Organizational Dynamics*, 16 (1): 34–43.

Cahn, M. 1978. OD at Saga: An Interview with William J. Crockett. *Journal of Applied Behavioral Science*, 14 (2): 223–235.

Chambless, D., and Goldstein, A. 1979. Behavioral Psychotherapy. In Corsini, R. (ed.) *Current Psychotherapies*, 2nd ed. 230–272. Itasca, IL: F. E. Peacock.

Church, A., Burke, W., and Van Eynde, D. 1994. Values, Motives, and Interventions of Organization Development Practitioners. *Group and Organization Management* 19 (1): 5–50.

Connellan, T. 1978. *How to Improve Human Performance: Behaviorism in Business and Industry*. New York: Harper and Row.

Connelly, S. 1984. *Work Spirit: Recapturing the Vitality of Work.* Doctoral Dissertation, George Washington University. Washington, D.C.

Corsini, R., and Wedding, D. (Eds.), 2000. *Current Psychotherapies,* 6th ed. Itasca, IL: F. E. Peacock.

Covey, S. 1989. *The Seven Habits of Highly Effective People: Restoring the Character Ethic.* New York: Simon & Schuster.

Cummings, T., and Worley, C. 2015. *Organization Development and Change,* 10th ed. Stamford, CT: Engage Learning.

Durant, W. 1953. *The Story of Philosophy.* New York: Pocket Books.

Ellis, A. 1979. Rational-Emotive Therapy. In Corsini R. (ed.) *Current Psychotherapies,* 2nd ed. 185–229. Itasca, IL: F. E. Peacock.

_____. 2001. *Overcoming Destructive Beliefs, Feelings, and Behaviors: New Directions for Rational Emotive Behavior Therapy.* Amherst, NY: Prometheus Books.

Fayol, H. 1949. *General and Industrial Administration.* London: Pittman & Sons.

Feldman, D., and Lankau, M. 2015. Executive Coaching: A Review and Agenda for Future Research. *Journal of Management,* 31: 829–848.

Ferguson, M. 1980. *The Aquarian Conspiracy: Personal and Social Transformation in the 1980s.* Los Angeles: J. P. Tarcher.

Filley, A., Foster, L., and Herbert, T. 1979. Teaching Organizational Behavior: Current Patterns and Implications. *Exchange, the Organizational Behavior Teaching Journal,* IV (2): 13–14.

Frankl, V. 1984. *Man's Search for Meaning.* New York: Washington Square Press/Pocket Books, Simon & Schuster.

French, W., and Bell, C. 1973. *Organizational Development: Behavioral Science Interventions for Organization Improvement.* Englewood Cliffs, NJ: Prentice Hall.

Fritjof, C. 1984. *The Tao of Physics,* 2nd ed. New York: Bantam Books.

George, B. 2003. *Authentic Leadership: Rediscovering the Secrets to Creating Lasting Value.* San Francisco: Jossey-Bass.

Goleman, D. 2006. *Emotional Intelligence: Why It Can Matter More than IQ.* 10th ed. New York: Bantam.

Goldsmith, M., and Lyons, L. 2005. Preface to the Second Edition. In Goldsmith, M., and Lyons, L. (Eds.) *Coaching for Leadership: The Practice of Leadership Coaching from the World's Greatest Coaches,* xviii–xxi. San Francisco: Pfeiffer.

Gowing, M., Kraft, J., and Quick J. (eds.) 1998. *The New Organizational Reality: Downsizing, Restructuring, and Revitalization.* Washington, D.C.: American Psychological Association.

Hammer, M., and Champy, J. 1993. *Reengineering the Corporation: A Manifesto for Business Revolution.* New York: Harper-Collins.

Hampton, D., Summer, C., and Weber R. 1973. *Organizational Behavior and the Practice of Management.* Glenview, IL: Scott Foresman & Company.

Hargrove, R. 1995. *Masterful Coaching: Extraordinary Results by Impacting People and the Way They Think and Act Together.* San Francisco: Jossey-Bass/Pfeiffer.

Harrison, R. 1984. Leadership and Strategy for a New Age. In Adams, J. (ed.) *Transforming Work,* 97–112. Alexandria, VA: Miles River Press.

Herman, S., and Korenich, M. 1977. *Authentic Management: A Gestalt Orientation to Organizations and Their Development.* Reading, MA: Addison-Wesley.

Hernez-Broome, G., and Hughes, R. 2004. Leadership Development: Past, Present, and Future. *Human Resource Planning,* 27 (1): 24–32.

Herrmann, N. 1995. *The Whole Brain Business Book.* New York: McGraw-Hill.

Herzberg, F. 1968. One More Time: How Do You Motivate Employees? *Harvard Business Review,* 46 (1): 53–62.

Huse, E. 1975. *Organization Development and Change.* St. Paul, MN: West Publishing Company.

International Humanist Ethical Union Bylaw 1.2. June 8, /http://iheu.org/about/organization/bylaws/.

Jamieson, D.W., and Rothwell, W. 2016. The Convergence of Organization Development and Human Resource Management. In Rothwell, W., Stavros, J., and Sullivan R. (Eds.) *Practicing Organization Development: Leading Transformation and Change,* 384–392. New York: Wiley.

Jensen, M. 2013. *HR Pioneers: A History of Human Resource Innovation at Control Data Corporation.* St. Cloud, MN: North Star Press.

Kaufmann, Y. 1979. Analytical Psychotherapy. In Corsini, R. (ed.) *Current Psychotherapies,* 2nd ed. 95–130. Itasca, IL: F. E. Peacock.

Kiefer, C., and Senge, P. 1984. Metanoic Organizations. In Adams, J. (ed.) *Transforming Work,* 69–84. Alexandria, VA: Miles River Press.

Kinlaw, D. 1996. *The ASTD Trainer's Sourcebook: Coaching.* New York: McGraw-Hill.

Kouzes, J., and Posner, B. 2015. When Leaders Are Coaches. In Goldsmith, M., and Lyons, L. (Eds.) *Coaching for Leadership: The Practice of Leadership Coaching from the World's Greatest Coaches,* 136–143. San Francisco: Pfeiffer.

Kuhn, T. 1996. *The Structure of Scientific Revolutions,* 3rd ed. Chicago: University of Chicago Press.

Lenberg, M. 1985, October 2. CDC Needs New Chief, Jacobs Says. *St. Paul Pioneer Press,* A-4.

Luthans, F. 1973. *Organizational Behavior.* New York: McGraw-Hill.

Luthans, F., and Kreitner, R. 1975. *Organizational Behavior Modification.* New York: Scott Foresman.

Maslow, A. 1968. *Toward a Psychology of Being.* New York: Van Nostrand.

Matoon, M. 1981. *Jungian Psychology in Perspective.* New York: The Free Press.

May, R. 2009. *Man's Search for Himself.* New York: W.W. Norton.

May, R., and Yalom, I. 2000. Existential Psychotherapy. In Corsini, R., and Wedding D. (Eds.) *Current Psychotherapies,* 6th ed. 273–302. Itasca, IL: F. E. Peacock.

McCall, M. and Lombardo, M. 1983. *Off the Track: Why and How Successful Executives Get Derailed, Technical Report 21.* Greensboro, NC: Center for Creative Leadership.

McCall, M., Lombardo, M., and Morrison, A. 1988. *The Lessons of Experience: How Successful Executives Develop on the Job.* New York: Lexington Books.

McCauley, C., Moxley, R., and Van Velsor, E. (Eds.), 1996. *The Center for Creative Leadership Handbook of Leadership Development.* San Francisco: Jossey-Bass.

McGregor, D. 1960. *The Human Side of Enterprise.* New York: McGraw-Hill.

Meador, D., and Rogers, C. 1979. Person-Centered Therapy. In Corsini R. (ed.) *Current Psychotherapies,* 2nd ed. 131–184. Itasca, IL: F. E. Peacock.

Minahan, M., and Crosby, R. 2016. The Classic T-Group. In Rothwell, W., Stavros, J., and Sullivan R. (Eds.) *Practicing Organization Development: Leading Transformation and Change,* 357–365. New York: Wiley.

Mosak, H. 1979. Adlerian Psychotherapy. In Corsini R. (ed.) *Current Psychotherapies,* 2nd ed. 44–95. Itasca, IL: F. E. Peacock.

Myatt, M. 2012. The #1 Reason Leadership Development Fails. Forbes.com, December 19. http://www.forbes.com/sites/mikemyatt/2012/12/19/the-1-reason-leadership-development-fails/#6b9c3b5934ce

Nelson, D., and Quick, J. 2006. *Organizational Behavior: Foundations, Realities & Challenges,* 5th ed. Mason, OH: Thomson South-Western.

Nicoll, D. 1998. Consulting to Organizational Transformations. In Adams, J. (ed.) *Transforming Work,* 2nd ed. 181–198. Alexandria, VA: Miles River Press.

Noer, D. 2006. *Coaching Behaviors Inventory Facilitators Guide, 2nd Ed.* Greensboro, NC: Noer Consulting.

_____. 2009. *Healing the Wounds: Overcoming the Trauma of Layoffs and Revitalizing Downsized Organizations.* San Francisco: Jossey-Bass.

_____. 2016. *Keeping Your Career on Track: Avoiding Derailment, Enhancing the Work Experience, and Helping Your Organization.* Jefferson, NC: McFarland.

Ohlott, P. 2004. Job Assignments. In McCauley, C., and Van Velsor, E. (Eds.) *The Center for Creative Leadership Handbook of Leadership Development,* 2nd ed. 183–203. San Francisco: Jossey-Bass.

Panza, C., and Gale, G. 2008. *Existentialism for Dummies.* New York: Wiley.

Porter, L. 1974. OD: Some Questions, Some Answers. *OD Practitioner,* 6 (3): 1–6.

_____. 1978. Some Extrapolations, Metaphors, and Inferential Leaps. *OD Practitioner,* 10 (3): 1–6.

Roethlisberger, F. 1977. *The Elusive Phenomena: An Autobiographical Account of My Work in the Field of Organizational Behavior at the Harvard Business School.* Boston: Harvard Business School.

Rogers, C. 1957. The Necessary and Sufficient Conditions of Therapeutic Personality Change. *Journal of Consulting and Clinical Psychology*, 21: 95–103.
_____. 1961. *On Becoming a Person*. Boston: Houghton-Mifflin.
Ross, R. 1994. The Ladder of Inference. In Senge, P., Kleiner, A., Roberts, C., Ross, R., and Smith, B. *The Fifth Discipline Fieldbook*. 242–246. New York: Doubleday.
Ross, R., Smith, B., Roberts, C., and Kleiner, A. 1994. Core Concepts About Learning in Organizations. In Senge, P., Kleiner, A., Roberts, C., Ross, R., and Smith, B. *The Fifth Discipline Fieldbook*, 48–50. New York: Doubleday.
Rost, J. 1991. *Leadership for the Twenty-First Century*. New York: Praeger.
Rothwell, W., Stavros, J., and Sullivan R. (Eds.) 2016 *Practicing Organization Development: Leading Transformation and Change*. New York: Wiley.
Schaef, A. 1986. *Co-Dependence: Misunderstood—Mistreated*. San Francisco: HarperCollins.
Schein, E., Bennis, W., and Beckhard, R. (Eds.) 1969. *Organization Development: Addison-Wesley Series*. Reading, MA: Addison-Wesley.
Scherer, J., Alban, B, and Weisbord, M. 2016. The Origins of Organization Development. In Rothwell, W., Stavros, J., and Sullivan R. (Eds.) *Practicing Organization Development: Leading Transformation and Change*, 26–41. New York: Wiley.
Seashore, C. 1999. What Is a T-Group? In Cooke, A., Brazzel, M., Craig, A., and Greig, B. (Eds.) *Reading Book for Human Relations*, 8th ed. 271–272. Silver Spring, MD: NTL Institute.
Senge, P. 1990. *The Fifth Discipline: The Art and Practice of the Learning Organization*. New York: Doubleday.
Senge, P., Kleiner, A., Roberts, C., Ross, R., and Smith, B. 1994. *The Fifth Discipline Fieldbook*. New York: Doubleday
Shank, J. 1997. *Team-Based Organizations: Developing a Successful Team Environment*. Chicago: Irwin.
Shaskin, M. 1981. Interview with Gordon Lippitt. *Group and Organizational Studies*, 6 (1): 18–24.
Simkin, J. 1979. Gestalt Therapy. In Corsini, R. (ed.) *Current Psychotherapies*, 2nd ed. 273–301. Itasca, IL: F. E. Peacock.
Skinner, B. 1953. *Science and Human Behavior*. New York: Macmillan.
_____. 1972. *Beyond Freedom and Dignity: A Stunning New Plan to Alter Human Behavior*, 3rd ed. New York: Bantam.
Sonnenfeld, J. 1985. The Case of Organization Study at Harvard: Stages in the Life of an Intellectual Community. *The Organizational Behavior Teaching Review*, IX (3): 31–51.
Strupp, H., and Hadley, S. 1977. A Tripartite Model of Mental Health and Therapeutic Outcomes. *American Psychologist*, 32 (3): 186–196.
Tannenbaum, R., and Davis, S. 1969. Values, Man, and Organizations. *Industrial Management Review*, 10 (2): 67–86.
_____. 1997. Of Time and the River. In Van Eynde, D., Hoy, J., and Van Eynde, D. (Eds.). *Organization Development Classics*, 171–175. San Francisco: Jossey-Bass.
Taylor, F. 1911. *The Principles of Scientific Management*. New York: Harper & Brothers.
Tillich, P. 1952. *The Courage to Be*. New Haven, CT: Yale University Press.
Ulrich, D. 1997. *Human Resource Champions: The Next Agenda for Adding Value and Delivering Results*. Cambridge, MA: Harvard Business School Press.
Vaill, P. 1984. Process Wisdom for a New Age. In Adams, J. (ed.) *Transforming Work*, 17–34. Alexandria, VA: Miles River Press.
_____. 1985. Integrating the Diverse Directions of the Behavioral Sciences. In Tannenbaum, R., Marguiles, N., and Massarik, F. (Eds.) *Human Systems Development*, 547–577. San Francisco: Jossey-Bass.
_____. 1989. *Management as a Performing Art*. San Francisco: Jossey-Bass.
_____. 2007. F. J. Roethlisberger and the Elusive Phenomena of Organizational Behavior. *Journal of Management Education*, 31 June: 321–338.
_____. 2009. *An Annotated Bibliography of Foundational Literature in Organizational Behavior and Development: Compiled with Commentary*. Minneapolis: Antioch University.
Van Eynde, D., Hoy, J., and Van Eynde, D.C. (eds.) 1997. *Organization Development Classics: The Practice and Theory of Change—The Best of* The OD Practitioner. San Francisco: Jossey-Bass.

Weisbord, M. 1977. How Do You Know It Works If You Don't Know What It Is? *OD Practitioner*, 9 (3): 1–8.

_____. 1983. The Cat in the Hat Breaks Through: Reflections on OD's Past, Present, and Future. *OD Practitioner*, 15 (1): 1–6.

_____. 1987. *Productive Workplaces: Organizing and Managing for Dignity, Meaning, and Community*. San Francisco: Jossey-Bass.

Whitworth, L., Kimsey-House, H., and Sandahl, P. 1998. *Co-Active Coaching: New Skills for Coaching People Toward Success in Work and Life*. Palo Alto, CA: Davies-Black.

Wilber, K. 1983. *Eye to Eye: The Quest for the New Paradigm*. New York: anchor Books.

Wolfe, T. 1979. *The Right Stuff*. New York: Farr, Straus, and Giroux.

Wolpe, J. 1973. *The Practice of Behavior Therapy*. New York: Pergamon Press.

Worley, C., and Feyerherm, A. 2003. Reflections on the Future of Organization Development. *The Journal of Applied Behavioral Science*, 39 (1): 97–115.

Index